perfect
indian

Bath · New York · Singapore · Hong Kong · Cologne · Delhi · Melbourne

This edition published by Parragon in 2008

Parragon Publishing
Queen Street House
4 Queen Street
Bath BA1 1HE, UK

Copyright © Parragon Books Ltd 2008
Cover by Talking Design
Designed by Terry Jeavons & Company
Additional text by Linda Doeser

ISBN: 978-1-4075-4827-2

Printed in China

Notes for the Reader
This book uses imperial, metric, and U.S. cup measurements. Follow the same units of measurement throughout; do not mix imperial and metric. All spoon measurements are level: teaspoons are assumed to be 5 ml, and tablespoons are assumed to be 15 ml. Unless otherwise stated, milk is assumed to be whole, eggs and individual vegetables, such as potatoes, are medium, and pepper is freshly ground black pepper.

The times given are an approximate guide only. Preparation times differ according to the techniques used by different people and the cooking times may also vary from those given as a result of the type of oven used. Optional ingredients, variations, or serving suggestions have not been included in the calculations.

Recipes using raw or very lightly cooked eggs should be avoided by infants, the elderly, pregnant women, convalescents, and anyone with a chronic condition. Pregnant and breastfeeding women are advised to avoid eating peanuts and peanut products. People with nut allergies should be aware that some of the prepared ingredients used in the recipes in this book may contain nuts. Always check the packaging before use.

perfect
indian

introduction

Nowadays supermarkets stock ingredients from across the world and city streets are lined with restaurants representing every imaginable country. In the West, Indian cooking is among the most popular of eastern cuisines, especially now that keen home cooks have discovered how easy it is to prepare authentic, tasty, and nutritious Indian dishes. Perhaps the secrets of its popularity are its subtlety and extraordinary variety.

Given that the subcontinent is so huge with an equally extensive history, it is hardly surprising that both its peoples and their diets are so diverse. Religious practices have had a profound influence—

Hindus don't eat beef, Muslims don't eat pork, and Buddhists, among others, are vegetarian. Explorers, conquerors, and colonizers have had an effect, too, clearly seen in the rich-tasting dishes created for Moghul emperors or the use of vinegar in the

curries of former Portuguese territories, for example. Foreign ingredients are most often seen in the dishes of western India. Climate and topography play their part and each region of the country has a unique style of cooking based on local ingredients. In the north, dairy products, such as yogurt and ghee (clarified butter), are featured, as well as nuts, while southern cooking is characterized by its use of coconuts, their oil, and a variety of chiles. Eastern regions are famous for their fish dishes and mustard oil. Delhi is well known for tandoori cooking, Kashmir for its meat, especially lamb, Madras for its wealth of vegetarian dishes, and Bengal for fine fish and tooth-achingly sweet desserts.

However, the cuisines of all regions are united in the use of

careful blends of spices, which are usually bought whole and ground as needed. These mixtures are subtle and aromatic but not invariably hot, although both fresh and dried chiles do feature in many dishes. With such a wide variety of choice, why not let Indian cuisine add a touch of spice to your culinary repertoire?

chicken

One of India's most popular meats, chicken is an excellent choice for curries and for cooking with subtle, aromatic spice blends. It can sometimes be rather bland, so combining it with other flavorsome ingredients, from almonds, garlic, and yogurt to onions, ginger, chiles, cumin, and coriander, turns it into a real feast. Indian cooks will often choose the dark meat, which tends to have more flavor, but diced chicken breast portions are ideal for stir-frying and can be substituted for thigh meat in other recipes according to taste.

Chicken is very versatile and is equally delicious roasted, braised, stir-fried, or broiled on skewers—all in Indian-style. It is frequently marinated, often only briefly, or rubbed with a dry spice mixture before cooking to give the dish a real depth of flavor. Because of its texture, it works especially well with creamy mixtures, such as the perennially popular chicken korma from northern India. It is also great in spicier curries that range from the fragrant and mild to the fiery hot. Added to this, it goes well with a wide range of accompaniments—plain boiled rice, dhals and other lentil dishes, Indian breads, and salads—so it's easy to add variety to the family menu.

chicken tikka masala

ingredients

SERVES 4–6

14 oz/400 g canned chopped
   tomatoes

1¹/₄ cups heavy cream

8 cooked tandoori chicken
   pieces (see page 32)

salt and pepper

fresh chopped cilantro,
   to garnish

cooked basmati rice, to serve

tikka masala

2 tbsp ghee, vegetable oil,
   or peanut oil

1 large garlic clove, finely
   chopped

1 fresh red chile, seeded and
   chopped

2 tsp ground cumin

2 tsp ground paprika

¹/₂ tsp salt

pepper

method

1 To make the tikka masala, melt the ghee in a large skillet with a lid over medium heat. Add the garlic and chile and stir-fry for 1 minute. Stir in the cumin, paprika, and salt and pepper to taste and continue stirring for about 30 seconds.

2 Stir the tomatoes and cream into the skillet. Reduce the heat to low and let the sauce simmer for about 10 minutes, stirring frequently, until it reduces and thickens.

3 Meanwhile, remove all the bones and any skin from the tandoori chicken pieces, then cut the meat into bite-size pieces.

4 Adjust the seasoning of the sauce, if necessary. Add the chicken pieces to the skillet, cover, and let simmer for 3–5 minutes, until the chicken is heated through. Garnish with cilantro and serve with cooked basmati rice.

chicken korma

ingredients

SERVES 4

1 chicken, weighing
    3 lb/1.3 kg
1 cup butter
3 onions, thinly sliced
1 garlic clove, crushed
1-inch/2.5-cm piece fresh
    ginger, grated
1 tsp mild chili powder
1 tsp ground turmeric
1 tsp ground coriander
$1/2$ tsp ground cardamom
$1/2$ tsp ground cinnamon
$1/2$ tsp salt
1 tbsp chickpea flour
$1/2$ cup milk
2 cups heavy cream
fresh cilantro leaves,
    to garnish
freshly cooked rice, to serve

method

1 Put the chicken into a large pan, cover with water, and bring to a boil. Reduce the heat, cover, and simmer for 30 minutes. Remove from the heat, lift out the chicken, and set aside to cool. Reserve $1/2$ cup of the cooking liquid. Remove and discard the skin and bones. Cut the flesh into bite-size pieces.

2 Heat the butter in a large pan over medium heat. Add the onions and garlic and cook, stirring, for 3 minutes, or until softened. Add the ginger, chili powder, turmeric, ground coriander, cardamom, cinnamon, and salt and cook for an additional 5 minutes. Add the chicken and the reserved cooking liquid. Cook for 2 minutes.

3 Blend the chickpea flour with a little of the milk and add to the pan, then stir in the remaining milk. Bring to a boil, stirring, then reduce the heat, cover, and simmer for 25 minutes. Stir in the cream, cover, and simmer for an additional 15 minutes.

4 Garnish with cilantro leaves and serve with freshly cooked rice.

kashmiri chicken

ingredients

SERVES 4–6

seeds from 8 green
    cardamom pods
$1/2$ tsp coriander seeds
$1/2$ tsp cumin seeds
1 cinnamon stick
8 black peppercorns
6 cloves
1 tbsp hot water
$1/2$ tsp saffron threads
3 tbsp ghee, vegetable oil,
    or peanut oil
1 large onion, finely chopped
2 tbsp garlic and ginger paste
generous 1 cup plain yogurt
8 skinless, boneless chicken
    thighs, sliced
3 tbsp ground almonds
generous $1/3$ cup blanched
    pistachios, finely chopped
2 tbsp chopped fresh cilantro
2 tbsp chopped fresh mint
salt
toasted slivered almonds,
    to garnish
Indian bread, to serve

method

1 Dry-roast the cardamom seeds in a skillet over medium–low heat, stirring continuously, until you can smell the aroma. Repeat with the coriander and cumin seeds, cinnamon stick, peppercorns, and cloves. Put all the spices, except the cinnamon stick, in a spice grinder, or use a pestle and grind to a powder.

2 Put the hot water and saffron threads in a small bowl and set aside.

3 Melt the ghee in a flameproof casserole over medium–high heat. Add the onion and sauté, stirring occasionally, for 5–8 minutes, until golden brown. Add the garlic and ginger paste and continue stirring for 2 minutes.

4 Stir in the ground spices and the cinnamon stick. Remove from the heat and mix in the yogurt, a small amount at a time, stirring vigorously with each addition, then return to the heat and continue stirring for 2–3 minutes, until the ghee separates. Add the chicken pieces.

5 Bring to a boil, stirring continuously, then reduce the heat to low, cover, and simmer for 20 minutes, stirring occasionally.

6 Stir in the ground almonds, pistachios, saffron with its soaking liquid, half the cilantro, all the mint, and salt to taste. Re-cover the casserole and continue simmering for about 5 minutes, until the chicken is tender and the sauce is thickened. Sprinkle with the remaining cilantro, garnish with slivered almonds, and serve with Indian bread.

chicken jalfrezi

ingredients

SERVES 4–6

4 tbsp ghee, vegetable oil, or peanut oil

8 skinless, boneless chicken thighs, sliced

1 large onion, chopped

2 tbsp garlic and ginger paste

2 green bell peppers, cored, seeded, and chopped

1 large fresh green chile, seeded and finely chopped

1 tsp ground cumin

1 tsp ground coriander

$1/4$–$1/2$ tsp chili powder

$1/2$ tsp ground turmeric

$1/4$ tsp salt

14 oz/400 g canned chopped tomatoes

$1/2$ cup water

chopped fresh cilantro, to garnish

method

1 Melt half the ghee in a wok or large skillet over medium–high heat. Add the chicken pieces and stir around for 5 minutes, until browned but not necessarily cooked through, then remove from the pan with a slotted spoon and set aside.

2 Melt the remaining ghee in the pan. Add the onion and sauté, stirring frequently, for 5–8 minutes, until golden brown. Stir in the garlic and ginger paste and continue sautéing for 2 minutes, stirring frequently.

3 Add the green bell peppers to the pan and stir around for 2 minutes.

4 Stir in the chile, cumin, coriander, chili powder, turmeric, and salt. Add the tomatoes with their juice and the water and bring to a boil.

5 Reduce the heat to low, add the chicken, and let simmer, uncovered, for 10 minutes, stirring frequently, until the bell peppers are tender, the chicken is cooked through, and the juices run clear if you pierce a few pieces with the tip of a knife. Sprinkle with the cilantro.

balti chicken

ingredients

SERVES 6

3 tbsp ghee or vegetable oil

2 large onions, sliced

3 tomatoes, sliced

$1/2$ tsp nigella seeds

4 black peppercorns

2 green cardamom pods

1 cinnamon stick

1 tsp chili powder

1 tsp garam masala

2 tsp garlic and ginger paste

1 lb 9 oz/700 g skinless,
   boneless chicken breasts
   or thighs, diced

2 tbsp plain yogurt

2 tbsp chopped fresh cilantro,
   plus extra sprigs to garnish

2 fresh green chiles, seeded
   and finely chopped

2 tbsp lime juice

salt

method

1 Heat the ghee in a large heavy-bottom skillet. Add the onions and cook over low heat, stirring occasionally, for 10 minutes, or until golden. Add the tomatoes, nigella seeds, peppercorns, cardamom pods, cinnamon stick, chili powder, garam masala, and garlic and ginger paste, and season to taste with salt. Cook, stirring constantly, for 5 minutes.

2 Add the chicken and cook, stirring constantly, for 5 minutes, or until well coated in the spice paste. Stir in the yogurt. Cover and let simmer, stirring occasionally, for 10 minutes.

3 Stir in the chopped cilantro, chiles, and lime juice. Transfer to a warmed serving dish, garnish with cilantro sprigs, and serve immediately.

butter chicken

ingredients

SERVES 4–6

1 onion, chopped

1$^1/_2$ tbsp garlic and ginger
    paste

14 oz/400 g canned chopped
    tomatoes

$^1/_4$–$^1/_2$ tsp chili powder

pinch of sugar

2 tbsp ghee, vegetable oil,
    or peanut oil

$^1/_2$ cup water

1 tbsp tomato paste

3 tbsp butter, cut into small
    pieces

$^1/_2$ tsp garam masala

$^1/_2$ tsp ground cumin

$^1/_2$ tsp ground coriander

8 cooked tandoori chicken
    pieces (see page 32)

4 tbsp heavy cream

salt and pepper

chopped cashew nuts and
    fresh cilantro sprigs,
    to garnish

method

1 Put the onion and the garlic and ginger paste in a food processor, blender, or spice grinder and process until a paste forms. Add the tomatoes, chili powder, sugar, and a pinch of salt and process again until blended.

2 Melt the ghee in a wok or large skillet over medium–high heat. Add the tomato mixture and water and stir in the tomato paste.

3 Bring the mixture to a boil, stirring, then reduce the heat to very low and simmer for 5 minutes, stirring occasionally, until the sauce thickens.

4 Stir in half the butter, the garam masala, cumin, and coriander. Add the chicken pieces and stir until they are well coated. Simmer for about an additional 10 minutes, or until the chicken is hot. Taste and adjust the seasoning, if necessary.

5 Lightly beat the cream in a small bowl and stir in several tablespoons of the hot sauce, beating continuously. Stir the cream mixture into the tomato sauce, then add the remaining butter and stir until it melts. Garnish with the chopped cashew nuts and cilantro sprigs and serve straight from the wok.

wok-cooked chicken in tomato & fenugreek sauce

ingredients

SERVES 4

1 lb 9 oz/700 g skinless,
    boneless chicken thighs,
    cut into 1-inch/2.5-cm
    cubes
juice of 1 lime
1 tsp salt, or to taste
4 tbsp sunflower oil or olive oil
1 large onion, finely chopped
2 tsp ginger paste
2 tsp garlic paste
$1/2$ tsp ground turmeric
$1/2$–1 tsp chili powder
1 tbsp ground coriander
15 oz/425 g canned chopped
    tomatoes
$1/2$ cup warm water
1 tbsp dried fenugreek leaves
$1/2$ tsp garam masala
2 tbsp chopped fresh cilantro
    leaves
2–4 fresh green chiles
Indian bread, to serve

method

1 Place the chicken in a nonmetallic bowl and rub in the lime juice and salt. Cover and set aside for 30 minutes.

2 Heat the oil in a wok or heavy skillet over medium–high heat. Add the onion and stir-fry for 7–8 minutes, until it begins to color.

3 Add the ginger and garlic pastes and continue to stir-fry for about a minute. Add the turmeric, chili powder, and ground coriander, then reduce the heat slightly and cook the spices for 25–30 seconds. Add half the tomatoes, stir-fry for 3–4 minutes, and add the remaining tomatoes. Continue to cook, stirring, until the tomato juice has evaporated and the oil separates from the spice paste and floats on the surface.

4 Add the chicken and increase the heat to high. Stir-fry for 4–5 minutes, then add the warm water, reduce the heat to medium–low, and cook for 8–10 minutes, or until the sauce has thickened and the chicken is tender.

5 Add the fenugreek leaves, garam masala, half the cilantro leaves, and the chiles. Cook for 1–2 minutes, remove from the heat, and transfer to a serving plate. Garnish with the remaining cilantro and serve with Indian bread.

chicken with stir-fried spices

ingredients

SERVES 4

1 lb 9 oz/700 g skinless,
    boneless chicken breasts
    or thighs

juice of $1/2$ lemon

1 tsp salt, or to taste

5 tbsp sunflower oil or olive oil

1 large onion, finely chopped

2 tsp garlic paste

2 tsp ginger paste

$1/2$ tsp ground turmeric

1 tsp ground cumin

2 tsp ground coriander

$1/2$–1 tsp chili powder

$5 1/2$ oz/150 g canned
    chopped tomatoes

$2/3$ cup warm water

1 large garlic clove, finely
    chopped

1 small or $1/2$ large red bell
    pepper, seeded and cut
    into 1-inch/2.5-cm pieces

1 small or $1/2$ large green bell
    pepper, seeded and cut
    into 1-inch/2.5-cm pieces

1 tsp garam masala

Indian bread, to serve

method

1 Cut the chicken into 1-inch/2.5-cm cubes and put in a nonmetallic bowl. Add the lemon juice and half the salt and rub well into the chicken. Cover and let marinate in the refrigerator for 20 minutes.

2 Heat 4 tablespoons of the oil in a medium heavy-bottom saucepan over medium heat. Add the onion and cook, stirring frequently, for 8–9 minutes, until lightly browned. Add the garlic and ginger pastes and cook, stirring, for 3 minutes. Add the turmeric, cumin, coriander, and chili powder and cook, stirring, for 1 minute. Add the tomatoes and their juice and cook for 2–3 minutes, stirring frequently, until the oil separates from the spice paste.

3 Add the marinated chicken, increase the heat slightly, and cook, stirring, until it changes color. Add the warm water and bring to a boil. Reduce the heat, cover, and simmer for 25 minutes.

4 Heat the remaining 1 tablespoon of oil in a small saucepan or skillet over low heat. Add the garlic and cook, stirring frequently, until browned. Add the bell peppers, increase the heat to medium, and stir-fry for 2 minutes, then stir in the garam masala. Fold the bell pepper mixture into the curry. Remove from the heat and serve immediately with Indian bread.

cumin-scented chicken

ingredients

SERVES 4

1 lb 9 oz/700 g boneless
   chicken thighs or breasts,
   cut into 5-cm/2-inch
   pieces
juice of 1 lime
1 tsp salt, or to taste
3 tbsp sunflower oil or olive oil
1 tsp cumin seeds
1-inch/2.5-cm piece
   cinnamon stick
5 green cardamom pods,
   bruised
4 cloves
1 large onion, finely chopped
2 tsp garlic paste
2 tsp ginger paste
$1/2$ tsp ground turmeric
2 tsp ground cumin
$1/2$ tsp chili powder
8 oz/225 g canned chopped
   tomatoes
1 tbsp tomato paste
$1/2$ tsp sugar
1 cup warm water
$1/2$ tsp garam masala
2 tbsp chopped fresh cilantro
   leaves, plus extra sprigs to
   garnish
Indian bread, to serve

method

1 Put the chicken in a nonmetallic bowl and rub in the lime juice and salt. Cover and set aside for 30 minutes.

2 Heat the oil in a medium saucepan over low heat and add the cumin seeds, cinnamon, cardamom, and cloves. Let them sizzle for 25–30 seconds, then add the onion. Cook, stirring frequently, for 5 minutes, or until the onion has softened.

3 Add the garlic paste and ginger paste and cook for about a minute, then add the turmeric, ground cumin, and chili powder. Add the tomatoes, tomato paste, and sugar. Cook over medium heat, stirring frequently, until the tomatoes reach a pastelike consistency and the oil separates from the spice paste. Sprinkle over a little water if the mixture sticks to the pan.

4 Add the chicken and increase the heat to medium–high. Stir until the chicken changes color, then pour in the warm water. Bring to a boil, reduce the heat to medium–low, and cook for 12–15 minutes, or until the sauce has thickened and the chicken is tender.

5 Stir in the garam masala and chopped cilantro. Transfer to a serving dish and garnish with cilantro sprigs. Serve with Indian bread.

chicken in green chile, mint & cilantro sauce

ingredients

SERVES 4

1/2 cup coarsely chopped fresh cilantro leaves and stalks

1 1/2 cups coarsely chopped fresh spinach

1-inch/2.5-cm piece fresh ginger, coarsely chopped

3 garlic cloves, coarsely chopped

2–3 fresh green chiles, coarsely chopped

1/4 cup fresh mint leaves

1 1/2 tbsp lemon juice

1/2 tsp salt, or to taste

1/3 cup plain yogurt

4 tbsp sunflower oil or olive oil

1 large onion, finely chopped

1 lb 9 oz/700 g skinless chicken thighs or breast portions, cut into 1-inch/ 2.5-cm cubes

1 tsp ground turmeric

1/2 tsp sugar

1 small tomato, seeded and cut into julienne strips, to garnish

cooked basmati rice, to serve

method

1 Place the cilantro, spinach, ginger, garlic, chiles, mint, lemon juice, and the 1/2 teaspoon of salt in a food processor or blender and process to a smooth paste. Add a little water, if necessary, to facilitate blade movement in a blender. Remove and set aside.

2 Whisk the yogurt until smooth (this is important because otherwise the yogurt will curdle) and set aside.

3 Heat the oil in a medium saucepan and cook the onion for 5–6 minutes, stirring frequently, until softened.

4 Add the chicken and stir-fry over medium–high heat for 2–3 minutes, until the meat turns opaque. Add the turmeric and sugar, with a little more salt if necessary, and stir-fry for an additional 2 minutes, then reduce the heat to medium, and add half the yogurt. Cook for 1 minute and add the remaining yogurt, then continue cooking over medium heat until the yogurt resembles a thick batter and the oil is visible.

5 Add the herb and spice mixture and cook for 4–5 minutes, stirring continuously. Remove from the heat and garnish with the strips of tomato. Serve with cooked basmati rice.

quick chicken curry with mushrooms & beans

ingredients

SERVES 4

4 tbsp ghee, vegetable oil,
   or peanut oil
8 skinless, boneless chicken
   thighs, sliced
1 small onion, chopped
2 large garlic cloves, crushed
$3^{1}/_{2}$ oz/100 g green beans,
   trimmed and chopped
generous $1^{3}/_{4}$ cups thickly
   sliced mushrooms
2 tbsp milk
salt and pepper
fresh cilantro sprigs,
   to garnish
cooked basmati rice, to serve

curry paste

2 tsp garam masala
1 tsp mild, medium, or hot
   curry powder, to taste
1 tbsp water

method

1 To make the curry paste, put the garam masala and curry powder in a bowl and stir in the water, then set aside.

2 Melt half the ghee in a large heavy-bottom pan or skillet with a tight-fitting lid over medium–high heat. Add the chicken and curry paste and stir around for 5 minutes.

3 Add the onion, garlic, and green beans and continue cooking for an additional 5 minutes, until the chicken is cooked through and the juices run clear.

4 Add the remaining ghee and the mushrooms and, when the ghee melts, stir in the milk. Season to taste with salt and pepper. Reduce the heat to low, cover, and simmer for 10 minutes, stirring occasionally. Garnish with cilantro sprigs and serve with cooked basmati rice.

chicken biryani

ingredients

SERVES 8

1 1/2 tsp finely chopped fresh
    ginger

1 1/2 tsp crushed garlic

1 tbsp garam masala

1 tsp chili powder

2 tsp salt

1 1/4 cups plain yogurt

5 green cardamom pods,
    bruised

1 chicken, weighing
    3 lb 5 oz/1.5 kg

2/3 cup milk

1 tsp saffron strands

6 tbsp ghee

2 onions, sliced

1 lb/450 g basmati rice

2 cinnamon sticks

4 fresh green chiles

4 tbsp lemon juice

2 tbsp cilantro leaves

method

1 Mix the ginger, garlic, garam masala, chili powder, half the salt, the yogurt, and the cardamom pods in a bowl. Skin and cut the chicken into 8 pieces, add to the spices, and mix well. Cover and marinate in the refrigerator for 3 hours.

2 Boil the milk in a small saucepan, sprinkle over the saffron, and set aside.

3 Heat the ghee in a saucepan. Add the onions and cook until golden. Transfer half of the onions and ghee to a bowl and set aside.

4 Place the rice and cinnamon sticks in a saucepan of water. Bring the rice to a boil and simmer for 4–5 minutes, then remove from the heat. Drain and place in a bowl. Mix with the remaining salt.

5 Chop the chiles and set aside. Add the chicken mixture to the pan containing the onions. Add half each of the chopped green chiles, lemon juice, cilantro, and saffron milk. Add the rice, then the rest of the ingredients, including the reserved onions and ghee. Cover tightly. Cook over low heat for 1 hour. Check that the meat is cooked through; if it is not cooked, return to the heat, and cook for an additional 15 minutes. Mix well before serving.

tandoori chicken

ingredients

SERVES 4

4 chicken pieces, about 8 oz/
225 g each, skinned

juice of $1/2$ lemon

$1/2$ tsp salt, or to taste

$1/3$ cup strained, whole-milk
plain yogurt or Greek-style
yogurt

3 tbsp heavy cream

1 tbsp chickpea flour

1 tbsp garlic paste

1 tbsp ginger paste

$1/2$–1 tsp chili powder

1 tsp ground coriander

$1/2$ tsp ground cumin

$1/2$ tsp garam masala

$1/2$ tsp ground turmeric

2 tbsp vegetable oil,
for brushing

3 tbsp melted butter or
olive oil

salad, to serve

lemon wedges, to garnish

method

1 Make 2–3 small incisions in each chicken piece and place in a large nonmetallic bowl. Rub in the lemon juice and salt, cover, and let marinate in the refrigerator for 20 minutes.

2 Meanwhile, put the yogurt in a separate bowl and add the cream and chickpea flour. Beat with a fork until well blended and smooth. Add all the remaining ingredients, except the oil and melted butter, and mix thoroughly. Pour over the chicken and rub in well. Cover and chill in the refrigerator for 4–6 hours, or overnight. Return to room temperature before cooking.

3 Preheat the broiler to high. Line a broiler pan with foil and brush the rack with oil. Using tongs, lift the chicken pieces out of the marinade and put on the prepared rack, reserving the remaining marinade. Cook the chicken for 4 minutes, then turn over and cook for an additional 4 minutes. Baste the chicken generously with the reserved marinade and cook for an additional 2 minutes on each side.

4 Brush the chicken with the melted butter and cook for 5–6 minutes, or until charred in patches. Turn over and baste with the remaining marinade. Cook for an additional 5–6 minutes, or until charred, tender, and the juices run clear when a skewer is inserted into the thickest part of the meat.

5 Transfer the chicken to a dish. Serve with salad and garnish with lemon wedges.

silky chicken kabobs

ingredients

SERVES 8

1/3 cup raw cashews

2 tbsp light cream

1 egg

1 lb/450 g skinless, boneless
chicken breasts, coarsely
chopped

1/2 tsp salt, or to taste

2 tsp garlic paste

2 tsp ginger paste

2 fresh green chiles, coarsely
chopped (seeded if
you like)

1 cup fresh cilantro, including
the tender stalks, coarsely
chopped

1 tsp garam masala

vegetable oil, for brushing

2 tbsp butter, melted

chutney, to serve

method

1 Put the cashews in a heatproof bowl, cover with boiling water, and let soak for 20 minutes. Drain and put in a food processor. Add the cream and egg and process the ingredients to a coarse mixture.

2 Add all the remaining ingredients, except the oil and melted butter, and process until smooth. Transfer to a bowl, cover, and let chill in the refrigerator for 30 minutes.

3 Preheat the broiler to high. Brush the rack and 8 metal or presoaked wooden skewers lightly with oil. Have a bowl of cold water ready.

4 Divide the chilled mixture into 8 equal-size portions. Dip your hands into the bowl of cold water—this will stop the mixture from sticking to your fingers when you are molding it onto the skewers. Carefully mold each portion onto a skewer, forming it into a 6-inch/15-cm sausage shape. Arrange the kabobs on the prepared rack and cook for 4 minutes. Brush with half the melted butter and cook for an additional minute. Turn over and cook for 3 minutes. Baste with the remaining melted butter and cook for an additional 2 minutes.

5 Remove from the heat and let the kabobs rest for 5 minutes before sliding them off the skewers with a knife. Serve with chutney.

creamy chicken tikka

ingredients

SERVES 4

1 lb 9 oz/700 g skinless,
   boneless chicken breasts,
   cut into 1-inch/2.5-cm
   cubes
2 tbsp lemon juice
$1/2$ tsp salt, or to taste
$1/2$ cup strained, whole-milk
   plain yogurt, or Greek-style
   yogurt
3 tbsp heavy cream
$1/4$ cup grated mild cheddar
   cheese
1 tbsp garlic paste
1 tbsp ginger paste
$1/2$–1 tsp chili powder
$1/2$ tsp ground turmeric
$1/2$ tsp sugar
1 tbsp chickpea flour, sifted
1 tsp garam masala
2 tbsp sunflower oil or
   olive oil, plus 2 tbsp
   for brushing
3 tbsp melted butter or
   olive oil
salad and chutney, to serve

method

1 Put the chicken in a nonmetallic bowl and add the lemon juice and salt. Rub well into the chicken. Cover and let marinate in the refrigerator for 20–30 minutes.

2 Put the yogurt in a separate nonmetallic bowl and beat with a fork until smooth. Add all the remaining ingredients, except the melted butter. Beat well until the ingredients are fully incorporated. Add the chicken and mix thoroughly until fully coated with the marinade. Cover and let marinate in the refrigerator for 4–6 hours, or overnight. Return to room temperature before cooking.

3 Preheat the broiler to high. Brush 6 metal skewers generously with the remaining 2 tablespoons of oil and thread on the chicken cubes. Brush over any remaining marinade. Place the prepared skewers in a broiler pan and broil about 3 inches/7.5 cm below the heat source for 4–5 minutes. Brush generously with the melted butter and cook for an additional 1–2 minutes. Turn over and cook for 3–4 minutes, basting frequently with the remaining melted butter.

4 Balance the skewers over a large saucepan or skillet and let rest for 5–6 minutes before sliding the chicken cubes off the skewers with a knife. Serve with salad and chutney.

meat

Because India was historically a poor country, meat dishes did not feature in the everyday menus of ordinary people but were usually served only on special occasions or in the homes of the rich. As a result, they are particularly succulent, thoughtfully spiced, and exceptionally delicious.

Mutton or lamb is far and away the most commonly eaten meat in India and it is prepared in a wide variety of ways in the different regions of this vast country—marinated and served in a fragrant yogurt sauce, ground and shaped into meatballs or koftas, curried with a variety of vegetables, or delicately spiced and broiled on skewers. Indian ways with lamb chops are so different from those in western kitchens that, if you haven't already tried them, these recipes simply must be explored.

Pork is the second most popular meat and recipes often show the culinary influence of foreigners. For example, the fiery hot vindaloo, with its distinctive and unique flavoring of spices and vinegar, originated in what was once Portuguese Goa.

Beef is less commonly used in India but features in Muslim cooking, with many of the dishes originating in the south of the country. Perhaps the most famous of these is the robust Madras curry.

lamb rogan josh

ingredients

SERVES 4

1$^1/_2$ cups plain yogurt

$^1/_2$ tsp ground asafetida,
   dissolved in 2 tbsp water

1 lb 9 oz/700 g boneless leg
   of lamb, trimmed and cut
   into 2-inch/5-cm cubes

2 tomatoes, seeded and
   chopped

1 onion, chopped

2 tbsp ghee, vegetable oil,
   or peanut oil

1$^1/_2$ tbsp garlic and ginger
   paste

2 tbsp tomato paste

2 bay leaves

1 tbsp ground coriander

$^1/_4$–1 tsp chili powder, ideally
   Kashmiri chili powder

$^1/_2$ tsp ground turmeric

1 tsp salt

$^1/_2$ tsp garam masala

method

1 Put the yogurt in a large bowl and stir in the dissolved asafetida. Add the lamb and use your hands to rub in all the marinade, then set aside for 30 minutes.

2 Meanwhile, put the tomatoes and onion in a food processor or blender and process until blended. Melt the ghee in a flameproof casserole or large skillet with a tight-fitting lid. Add the garlic and ginger paste and stir until the aromas are released.

3 Stir in the tomato mixture, tomato paste, bay leaves, coriander, chili powder, and turmeric, reduce the heat to low, and simmer, stirring occasionally, for 5–8 minutes.

4 Add the lamb and salt with any leftover marinade and stir for 2 minutes. Cover, reduce the heat to low, and simmer, stirring occasionally, for 30 minutes. The lamb should give off enough moisture to prevent it from catching on the bottom of the skillet, but if the sauce looks too dry, stir in a little water.

5 Sprinkle with the garam masala, re-cover the skillet, and continue simmering for 15–20 minutes, until the lamb is tender. Serve immediately.

peshawar-style lamb curry

ingredients

SERVES 4

4 tbsp sunflower oil or olive oil

1-inch/2.5-cm piece
   cinnamon stick

5 green cardamom pods,
   bruised

5 cloves

2 bay leaves

1 lb 9 oz/700 g boneless leg
   of lamb, cut into 1-inch/
   2.5-cm cubes

1 large onion, finely chopped

2 tsp garlic paste

2 tsp ginger paste

1 tbsp tomato paste

1 tsp ground turmeric

1 tsp ground coriander

1 tsp ground cumin

generous $1/2$ cup thick plain
   yogurt

2 tsp chickpea flour or
   cornstarch

$1/2$–1 tsp chili powder

$2/3$ cup warm water

1 tbsp chopped fresh mint
   leaves

2 tbsp chopped fresh cilantro
   leaves

Indian bread, to serve

method

1 In a medium saucepan, heat the oil over low heat and add the cinnamon, cardamom, cloves, and bay leaves. Let them sizzle for 25–30 seconds, then add the meat, increase the heat to medium–high, and cook until the meat begins to brown and all the natural juices have evaporated.

2 Add the onion and garlic and ginger pastes and cook for 5–6 minutes, stirring frequently, then add the tomato paste, turmeric, coriander, and cumin. Continue to cook for 3–4 minutes.

3 Whisk together the yogurt, chickpea flour, and chili powder and add to the meat. Reduce the heat to low, add the warm water, cover, and simmer, stirring frequently to make sure that the sauce does not stick to the bottom of the pan, for 45–50 minutes, until the meat is tender. Simmer, uncovered, if necessary to thicken the sauce to the desired consistency.

4 Stir in the fresh mint and cilantro, remove from the heat, and serve with Indian bread.

lamb dopiaza

ingredients

SERVES 4

4 onions, sliced into rings

3 garlic cloves, coarsely
chopped

1-inch/2.5-cm piece fresh
ginger, grated

1 tsp ground coriander

1 tsp ground cumin

1 tsp chili powder

$1/2$ tsp ground turmeric

1 tsp ground cinnamon

1 tsp garam masala

4 tbsp water

5 tbsp butter or vegetable oil

1 lb 8 oz/680 g boneless
lamb, cut into bite-size
chunks

6 tbsp plain yogurt

salt and pepper

fresh cilantro leaves,
to garnish

cooked basmati rice, to serve

method

1 Put half of the onion rings into a food processor with the garlic, ginger, ground coriander, cumin, chili powder, turmeric, cinnamon, and garam masala. Add the water and process to a paste.

2 Heat 4 tablespoons of the butter in a pan over medium heat. Add the remaining onions and cook, stirring, for 3 minutes. Remove from the heat. Lift out the onions with a slotted spoon and set aside. Heat the remaining butter in the pan over high heat, add the lamb, and cook, stirring, for 5 minutes. Lift out the meat and drain on paper towels.

3 Add the onion paste to the pan and cook over medium heat, stirring, until the oil separates. Stir in the yogurt, season to taste with salt and pepper, return the lamb to the pan, and stir well.

4 Bring the mixture gently to a boil, reduce the heat, cover, and simmer for 25 minutes. Stir in the reserved onion rings and cook for an additional 5 minutes. Remove from the heat and garnish with cilantro leaves. Serve immediately with cooked basmati rice.

lamb & spinach curry

ingredients

SERVES 2–4

$1^1/_4$ cups vegetable oil

2 onions, sliced

2 tbsp chopped fresh cilantro

2 fresh green chiles, chopped

$1^1/_2$ tsp finely chopped fresh
    ginger

$1^1/_2$ tsp crushed garlic

1 tsp chili powder

$^1/_2$ tsp ground turmeric

1 lb/450 g lean lamb, cut into
    bite-size chunks

1 tsp salt

2 lb 4 oz/1 kg fresh spinach,
    trimmed, washed, and
    chopped

3 cups water

finely chopped fresh red
    chile, to garnish

method

1 Heat the oil in a large heavy-bottom skillet. Add the onions and cook until golden.

2 Add the fresh cilantro and green chiles to the skillet and stir-fry for 3–5 minutes. Reduce the heat and add the ginger, garlic, chili powder, and turmeric, stirring well.

3 Add the lamb to the skillet and stir-fry for an additional 5 minutes. Add the salt and the spinach and cook, stirring occasionally with a wooden spoon, for an additional 3–5 minutes.

4 Add the water, stirring, and cook over low heat, covered, for 45 minutes. Remove the lid and check the meat. If it is not tender, turn the meat over, increase the heat, and cook, uncovered, until the surplus water has been absorbed. Stir-fry the mixture for an additional 5–7 minutes.

5 Transfer the lamb and spinach mixture to a warmed serving dish and garnish with chopped red chile. Serve hot.

lamb with cauliflower

ingredients

SERVES 4

2 tbsp ghee, vegetable oil,
     or peanut oil
1 onion, chopped
$1/2$ tbsp garlic and ginger
     paste
1 tbsp cumin seeds
2 tsp mild, medium, or hot
     curry paste, to taste
1 head cauliflower, broken
     into small florets
14 oz/400 g canned chopped
     tomatoes
$1/2$ cup vegetable stock or
     water
1 lb 9 oz/700 g lamb neck
     fillet, trimmed and cut into
     $1/4$-inch/5-mm slices
lemon juice, to taste
salt and pepper
chopped fresh mint,
     to garnish

method

1 Melt the ghee in a wok or large skillet over medium–high heat. Add the onion and garlic and ginger paste and sauté, stirring frequently, for 5–8 minutes, until the onion is lightly browned.

2 Add the cumin seeds and curry paste and stir around for about 1 minute. Add the cauliflower and continue stirring for an additional minute.

3 Add the tomatoes with their juice, the stock, and salt and pepper to taste. Bring to a boil, then reduce the heat and simmer for 10 minutes, stirring occasionally, until the sauce is reduced and the tomatoes break down.

4 Add the lamb and continue simmering, stirring occasionally, for 10 minutes, or until it is tender and just pink in the center. Add lemon juice to taste and adjust the seasoning, if necessary. Serve garnished with a generous amount of mint.

lamb pasanda

ingredients

SERVES 4–6

1 lb 5 oz/600 g boneless
    shoulder or leg of lamb

2 tbsp garlic and ginger paste

4 tbsp ghee, vegetable oil,
    or peanut oil

3 large onions, chopped

1 fresh green chile, seeded
    and chopped

2 green cardamom pods,
    bruised

1 cinnamon stick, broken
    in half

2 tsp ground coriander

1 tsp ground cumin

1 tsp ground turmeric

generous 1 cup water

$2/3$ cup heavy cream

4 tbsp ground almonds

$1^1/_2$ tsp salt

1 tsp garam masala

paprika and toasted slivered
    almonds, to garnish

method

1 Cut the meat into thin slices, then place the slices between plastic wrap and pound with a meat mallet to make them even thinner. Put the lamb slices in a bowl, add the garlic and ginger paste, and rub well into the lamb. Cover and let marinate in the refrigerator for 2 hours.

2 Melt the ghee in a large skillet over medium–high heat. Add the onions and chile and sauté, stirring frequently, for 5–8 minutes, until golden brown.

3 Stir in the cardamom pods, cinnamon stick, ground coriander, cumin, and turmeric and continue stirring for 2 minutes, or until the spices are aromatic.

4 Add the meat to the skillet and cook, stirring occasionally, for about 5 minutes, until it is browned on all sides and the fat begins to separate. Stir in the water and bring to a boil, still stirring. Reduce the heat to its lowest setting, cover the skillet tightly, and simmer for 40 minutes, or until the meat is tender.

5 Mix the cream and ground almonds together in a bowl. Beat in 6 tablespoons of the hot cooking liquid from the skillet, then gradually beat this mixture back into the skillet. Stir in the salt and garam masala. Continue to simmer for an additional 5 minutes, uncovered, stirring occasionally.

6 Garnish with a sprinkling of paprika and slivered almonds and serve.

meatballs in creamy cashew nut sauce

ingredients

SERVES 4

1 lb/450 g fresh lean ground
    lamb

1 tbsp thick plain yogurt

1 large egg, beaten

$^1/_2$ tsp ground cardamom

$^1/_2$ tsp ground nutmeg

$^1/_2$ tsp pepper

$^1/_2$ tsp dried mint

$^1/_2$ tsp salt, or to taste

$1^1/_4$ cups water

1-inch/2.5-cm piece
    cinnamon stick

5 green cardamom pods

5 cloves

2 bay leaves

3 tbsp sunflower oil or olive oil

1 onion, finely chopped

2 tsp garlic paste

1 tsp ground ginger

1 tsp ground fennel seeds

$^1/_2$ tsp ground turmeric

$^1/_2$–1 tsp chili powder

generous 1 cup raw cashews,
    soaked in $^2/_3$ cup boiling
    water for 20 minutes

$^2/_3$ cup heavy cream

1 tbsp crushed pistachios,
    to garnish

method

1 Put the lamb into a bowl and add the yogurt, egg, cardamom, nutmeg, pepper, mint, and salt. Knead the meat until it is smooth and velvety. Chill for 30–40 minutes, then divide into quarters. Make five balls out of each quarter and roll them between your palms to make them smooth and neat.

2 Bring the cold water to a boil in a large saucepan and add all the whole spices and the bay leaves. Add the meatballs in a single layer, reduce the heat to medium, cover the pan, and cook for 12–15 minutes. Remove the meatballs, cover, and keep hot. Strain the spiced stock and set aside.

3 Wipe out the pan and add the oil. Place over medium heat and add the onion and garlic paste. Cook until the mixture begins to brown and add the ground ginger, fennel, turmeric, and chili powder. Stir-fry for 2–3 minutes, then add the strained stock and meatballs. Bring to a boil, reduce the heat to low, cover, and simmer for 10–12 minutes.

4 Meanwhile, process the cashews to a paste in a blender and add to the meatball mixture along with the cream. Simmer for an additional 5–6 minutes, then remove from the heat. Garnish with crushed pistachios and serve.

lamb kabobs

ingredients

SERVES 4

$^1/_3$ cup raw cashews

3 tbsp heavy cream

1 egg

1 tbsp chickpea flour

2 fresh green chiles, coarsely
    chopped

2 shallots, coarsely chopped

1 lb/450 g fresh ground lamb

1 tsp salt, or to taste

2 tsp garlic paste

2 tsp ginger paste

1 tsp ground cumin

1 tsp garam masala

1 tbsp chopped fresh mint
    leaves

2 tbsp chopped fresh cilantro
    leaves

$^1/_2$ red bell pepper, finely
    chopped

2 tbsp vegetable oil,
    for brushing

4 tbsp butter, melted

salad and chutney, to serve

method

1 Put the cashews in a heatproof bowl, cover with boiling water, and let soak for 20 minutes. Drain and put in a food processor. Add the cream and egg and process the ingredients to a coarse mixture.

2 Add all the remaining ingredients, except the herbs, red bell pepper, oil, and butter, and process until thoroughly mixed. Transfer the mixture to a large bowl. Add the herbs and red bell pepper and mix well. Cover and chill in the refrigerator for 30–40 minutes.

3 Preheat the broiler to high. Brush the rack and 8 metal skewers lightly with oil. Have a bowl of cold water ready.

4 Divide the chilled mixture into 8 equal-size portions. Dip your hands into the bowl of cold water—this will stop the mixture from sticking to your fingers when you are molding it onto the skewer. Carefully mold each portion onto a skewer, forming it into a 6-inch/15-cm sausage shape. Arrange the kabobs on the prepared rack and cook for 4 minutes. Brush with half the melted butter and cook for an additional minute. Turn over and cook for 3 minutes. Baste with the remaining melted butter and cook for an additional 2 minutes.

5 Remove from the heat and let the kabobs rest for 5 minutes before sliding them off the skewers with a knife. Serve with salad and chutney.

kashmiri lamb chops

ingredients

SERVES 4

8 lamb chops

$1^{1}/_{4}$ cups whole milk

1 tbsp ginger paste

$^{1}/_{2}$ tsp pepper

pinch of saffron threads,
    pounded

$1^{1}/_{2}$ tsp ground fennel seeds

1 tsp ground cumin

$^{1}/_{2}$ tsp chili powder

4 cloves

1-inch/2.5-cm piece
    cinnamon stick

4 green cardamom pods,
    bruised

1 tsp salt, or to taste

$^{1}/_{2}$ tsp garam masala

1 tbsp fresh mint leaves,
    chopped, or $^{1}/_{2}$ tsp dried
    mint

1 tbsp chopped fresh cilantro
    leaves

mixed leaf salad, for serving

method

1 Remove the rind from the chops. Bring enough water to cover the chops to a boil in a medium saucepan. Add the chops, return to a boil, and cook for 2–3 minutes. Drain the chops, rinse, and drain again.

2 Put the drained chops into a large nonstick saucepan and add all the remaining ingredients, except the garam masala and herbs. Put the saucepan over medium heat and stir until the milk begins to bubble. Reduce the heat to low, cover, and cook for 30 minutes, turning the chops occasionally.

3 Remove from the heat. Using tongs, lift the chops out of the saucepan and shake the cooking liquid back into the saucepan. Strain the liquid and return to the saucepan with the chops. Cook over medium heat, turning frequently, for 7–8 minutes, until the liquid has evaporated and the chops are browned.

4 Sprinkle the garam masala evenly over the chops and add the mint and cilantro. Stir and cook for 1 minute. Serve immediately with a mixed salad.

sesame lamb chops

ingredients

SERVES 4

12 lamb chops, such as
    blade or rib
corn oil, for brushing
1$^{1}/_{2}$ tbsp sesame seeds
pepper and lime wedges,
    to serve

marinade

4 tbsp plain yogurt
2 tbsp grated lemon rind
1$^{1}/_{2}$ tsp ground cumin
1$^{1}/_{2}$ tsp ground coriander
$^{1}/_{4}$ tsp chili powder
salt

method

1 To make the marinade, put the yogurt, lemon rind, cumin, coriander, chili powder, and salt to taste in a large bowl and stir together.

2 Use a sharp knife to trim any fat from the edge of the lamb chops and scrape the meat off the long piece of bone. Using a rolling pin or the end of a large chef's knife, pound each chop until it is about $^{1}/_{4}$ inch/5 mm thick.

3 Add the chops to the bowl and use your hands to stir around until they are coated in the marinade. Let marinate for 20 minutes at room temperature, or cover the bowl and refrigerate for up to 4 hours. Return to room temperature before cooking.

4 Preheat the broiler to high and brush the broiler rack lightly with oil.

5 Arrange the chops on the broiler rack in a single layer, then sprinkle the sesame seeds over each. Broil the chops for about 7 minutes, without turning, for medium.

6 Grind fresh pepper over the chops and serve with lime wedges for squeezing over.

marinated lamb brochettes

ingredients

SERVES 4

1 lb 9 oz/700 g boned leg of
   lamb, cut into 1-inch/
   2.5-cm cubes

2 tbsp vinegar

$1/2$ tsp salt, or to taste

1 tbsp garlic paste

1 tbsp ginger paste

$1/2$ cup strained, whole-milk
   plain yogurt or Greek-style
   yogurt

1 tbsp chickpea flour

1 tsp ground cumin

1 tsp garam masala

$1/2$–1 tsp chili powder

$1/2$ tsp ground turmeric

3 tbsp olive oil or sunflower
   oil, plus 1 tbsp for
   brushing

$1/2$ red bell pepper, cut into
   1-inch/2.5-cm pieces

$1/2$ green bell pepper, cut into
   1-inch/2.5-cm pieces

8 shallots, halved

4 tbsp butter, melted

lemon wedges, to serve

method

1 Put the meat in a large nonmetallic bowl and add the vinegar, salt, and garlic and ginger pastes. Mix together thoroughly, cover, and let marinate in the refrigerator for 30 minutes.

2 Put the yogurt and chickpea flour in a separate bowl and beat together with a fork until smooth. Add the cumin, garam masala, chili powder, turmeric, and oil and mix together thoroughly. Add the yogurt mixture to the marinated meat, then add the bell peppers and shallots and stir until well blended. Cover and let marinate in the refrigerator for 2–3 hours, or overnight. Return to room temperature before cooking.

3 Preheat the broiler to high. Line the broiler pan with a piece of foil. Brush the rack and 4 metal skewers with the oil.

4 Thread the marinated lamb, bell peppers, and shallots alternately onto the prepared skewers. Place the skewers on the prepared rack and cook for 4 minutes. Brush generously with half the melted butter and cook for an additional 2 minutes. Turn over and cook for 3–4 minutes. Brush with the remaining butter and cook for an additional 2 minutes.

5 Balance the brochettes over a large saucepan or skillet and let rest for 5–6 minutes before sliding the lamb, bell peppers, and shallots off the skewers with a knife. Serve with the lemon wedges.

cilantro lamb kabobs

ingredients

SERVES 4–6

1 lb 9 oz/700 g ground lamb

1 onion, grated

3 tbsp finely chopped fresh
   cilantro, plus extra sprigs
   to garnish

3 tbsp finely chopped fresh
   mint

3 tbsp chickpea flour

$1^1/_2$ tbsp ground almonds

1-inch/2.5-cm piece fresh
   ginger, grated

3 tbsp lemon juice

2 tbsp plain yogurt

2 tsp ground cumin

2 tsp ground coriander

$1^1/_2$ tsp salt

$1^1/_2$ tsp garam masala

1 tsp ground cinnamon

pepper, to taste

vegetable oil, for brushing

lemon wedges, to serve

method

1 Place all the ingredients, except the oil, in a large bowl and use your hands to incorporate everything until the texture is smooth. Cover the bowl with a dish towel and let stand for about 45 minutes at room temperature.

2 With wet hands, divide the lamb mixture into 24 equal-size balls. Working with one ball at a time, mold it around a long, flat metal skewer. Continue until all the mixture has been used and you have filled 4–6 skewers.

3 Preheat the broiler to high. Lightly brush the broiler rack with oil. Add the skewers and broil for 5–7 minutes, turning frequently, until the lamb is completely cooked through and not at all pink when you pierce it with the point of a knife. Garnish with cilantro sprigs and serve with lemon wedges for squeezing over.

kheema matar

ingredients

SERVES 4–6

2 tbsp ghee, vegetable oil,
   or peanut oil

2 tsp cumin seeds

1 large onion, finely chopped

1 tbsp garlic and ginger paste

2 bay leaves

1 tsp mild, medium, or hot
   curry powder, to taste

2 tomatoes, seeded and
   chopped

1 tsp ground coriander

$1/4$–$1/2$ tsp chili powder

$1/4$ tsp ground turmeric

pinch of sugar

$1/2$ tsp salt

$1/2$ tsp pepper

1 lb 2 oz/500 g lean ground
   beef or lamb

$2^1/4$ cups frozen peas,
   straight from the freezer

method

1 Melt the ghee in a flameproof casserole or large skillet with a tight-fitting lid. Add the cumin seeds and cook, stirring, for 30 seconds, or until they start to crackle.

2 Stir in the onion, garlic and ginger paste, bay leaves, and curry powder and continue to stir-fry until the fat separates.

3 Stir in the tomatoes and cook for 1–2 minutes. Stir in the coriander, chili powder, turmeric, sugar, salt, and pepper and stir around for 30 seconds.

4 Add the beef and cook for 5 minutes, or until it is no longer pink, using a wooden spoon to break up the meat. Reduce the heat and simmer, stirring occasionally, for 10 minutes.

5 Add the peas and continue simmering for an additional 10–15 minutes, until the peas are thawed and hot. If there is too much liquid left in the casserole, increase the heat and let it bubble for a few minutes until it reduces.

balti beef

ingredients

SERVES 4–6

2 tbsp ghee, vegetable oil,
   or peanut oil
1 large onion, chopped
2 garlic cloves, crushed
2 large red bell peppers,
   seeded and chopped
1 lb 5 oz/600 g boneless
   beef, such as sirloin,
   thinly sliced
fresh cilantro sprigs,
   to garnish
Indian bread, to serve

balti sauce

2 tbsp ghee, vegetable oil,
   or peanut oil
2 large onions, chopped
1 tbsp garlic and ginger paste
14 oz/400 g canned chopped
   tomatoes
1 tsp ground paprika
$1/2$ tsp ground turmeric
$1/2$ tsp ground cumin
$1/2$ tsp ground coriander
$1/4$ tsp chili powder
$1/4$ tsp ground cardamom
1 bay leaf
salt and pepper

method

1 To make the balti sauce, melt the ghee in a wok or large skillet over medium–high heat. Add the onions and garlic and ginger paste and stir-fry for about 5 minutes, until the onions are golden brown. Stir in the tomatoes, then add the paprika, turmeric, cumin, coriander, chili powder, cardamom, bay leaf, and salt and pepper to taste. Bring to a boil, stirring, then reduce the heat and simmer for 20 minutes, stirring occasionally.

2 Let the sauce cool slightly, then remove the bay leaf and pour the mixture into a food processor or blender and process to a smooth sauce.

3 Wipe out the wok and return it to medium–high heat. Add the ghee and melt. Add the onion and garlic and stir-fry for 5–8 minutes, until golden brown. Add the bell peppers and continue stir-frying for 2 minutes.

4 Stir in the beef and continue stirring for 2 minutes, until it starts to turn brown. Add the balti sauce and bring to a boil. Reduce the heat and simmer for 5 minutes, or until the sauce slightly reduces again and the bell peppers are tender. Adjust the seasoning, if necessary. Garnish with cilantro sprigs and serve with Indian bread.

beef madras

ingredients

SERVES 4–6

1–2 dried red chiles

2 tsp ground coriander

2 tsp ground turmeric

1 tsp black mustard seeds

$^{1}/_{2}$ tsp ground ginger

$^{1}/_{4}$ tsp pepper

$1^{1}/_{4}$ cups coconut cream

4 tbsp ghee, vegetable oil,
    or peanut oil

2 onions, chopped

3 large garlic cloves, chopped

1 lb 9 oz/700 g lean braising
    beef, trimmed and cut into
    2-inch/5-cm cubes

generous 1 cup beef stock,
    plus a little extra if
    necessary

lemon juice

salt

pappadams, to serve

method

1 Depending on how hot you want this dish to be, chop the chiles with or without any seeds. The more seeds you include, the hotter the dish will be. Put the chopped chiles and any seeds in a small bowl with the coriander, turmeric, mustard seeds, ginger, and pepper and stir in a little of the coconut cream to make a thin paste.

2 Melt the ghee in a flameproof casserole or large skillet with a tight-fitting lid over medium–high heat. Add the onions and garlic and cook for 5–8 minutes, stirring frequently, until the onions are golden brown. Add the spice paste and stir for 2 minutes, or until you can smell the aromas.

3 Add the meat and stock and bring to a boil. Reduce the heat to its lowest level, cover tightly, and simmer for $1^{1}/_{2}$ hours, or until the beef is tender. Check occasionally that the meat isn't catching on the bottom of the casserole, and stir in a little extra water or stock, if necessary.

4 Uncover the casserole and stir in the remaining coconut cream with the lemon juice and salt to taste. Bring to a boil, stirring, then reduce the heat again and simmer, still uncovered, until the sauce reduces slightly. Serve with pappadams.

beef korma with almonds

ingredients

SERVES 6

1¼ cups vegetable oil

3 onions, finely chopped

2 lb 4 oz/1 kg lean beef,
    cubed

1½ tsp garam masala

1½ tsp ground coriander

1½ tsp finely chopped fresh
    ginger

1½ tsp crushed garlic

1 tsp salt

²/3 cup plain yogurt

2 whole cloves

3 green cardamom pods

4 black peppercorns

2½ cups water

chapatis, to serve

to garnish

chopped blanched almonds

sliced fresh green chiles

chopped fresh cilantro

method

1 Heat the oil in a large heavy-bottom skillet. Add the onions and stir-fry for 8–10 minutes, until golden. Remove half of the onions and set aside.

2 Add the meat to the remaining onions in the skillet and stir-fry for 5 minutes. Remove the skillet from the heat.

3 Mix the garam masala, coriander, ginger, garlic, salt, and yogurt together in a large bowl. Gradually add the meat to the yogurt-and-spice mixture and mix to coat the meat on all sides. Place the meat mixture in the skillet, return to the heat, and stir-fry for 5–7 minutes, or until the mixture is nearly brown.

4 Add the cloves, cardamom pods, and peppercorns. Add the water, reduce the heat, cover, and let simmer for 45–60 minutes. If the water has completely evaporated but the meat is still not tender enough, add another 1¼ cups water and cook for an additional 10–15 minutes, stirring occasionally.

5 Transfer to warmed serving dishes and garnish with the reserved onions, chopped almonds, chiles, and fresh cilantro. Serve with chapatis.

beef dhansak

ingredients

SERVES 6

2 tbsp ghee or vegetable oil

2 onions, chopped

3 garlic cloves, finely chopped

2 tsp ground coriander

2 tsp ground cumin

2 tsp garam masala

1 tsp ground turmeric

1 lb/450 g zucchini, peeled
  and chopped, or bitter
  gourd or pumpkin, peeled,
  seeded, and chopped

1 eggplant, peeled and
  chopped

4 curry leaves

generous 1 cup red split
  lentils (masoor dhal)

4 cups water

2 lb 4 oz/1 kg braising beef,
  diced

salt

fresh cilantro leaves,
  to garnish

method

1 Heat the ghee in a large heavy-bottom pan. Add the onions and garlic and cook over low heat, stirring occasionally, for 8–10 minutes, or until golden. Stir in the coriander, cumin, garam masala, and turmeric and cook, stirring constantly, for 2 minutes.

2 Add the zucchini, eggplant, curry leaves, lentils, and water. Bring to a boil, then reduce the heat, cover, and let simmer for 30 minutes, or until the vegetables are tender. Remove the pan from the heat and let cool slightly. Transfer the mixture to a food processor, in batches if necessary, and process until smooth. Return the mixture to the pan and season to taste with salt.

3 Add the beef to the pan and bring to a boil. Reduce the heat, cover, and let simmer for $1\frac{1}{4}$ hours. Remove the lid and continue to simmer for an additional 30 minutes, or until the sauce is thick and the beef is tender. Serve garnished with cilantro leaves.

pork vindaloo

ingredients

SERVES 4

2–6 dried red chiles, torn

5 cloves

1-inch/2.5-cm piece
  cinnamon stick, broken up

4 green cardamom pods

$1/2$ tsp black peppercorns

$1/2$ mace blade

$1/4$ nutmeg, lightly crushed

1 tsp cumin seeds

$1^1/2$ tsp coriander seeds

$1/2$ tsp fenugreek seeds

2 tsp garlic paste

1 tbsp ginger paste

3 tbsp cider vinegar or white
  wine vinegar

1 tbsp tamarind juice or juice
  of $1/2$ lime

1 lb 9 oz/700 g boneless leg
  of pork, cut into 1-inch/
  2.5-cm cubes

4 tbsp sunflower oil or olive
  oil, plus 2 tsp

2 large onions, finely chopped

generous 1 cup warm water,
  plus 4 tbsp

1 tsp salt, or to taste

1 tsp dark brown sugar

2 large garlic cloves, finely
  sliced

8–10 fresh or dried curry
  leaves

method

1 Grind the first ten ingredients (all the spices) to a fine powder in a spice grinder. Transfer the ground spices to a bowl and add the garlic and ginger pastes, vinegar, and tamarind juice. Mix together to form a paste.

2 Put the pork in a large nonmetallic bowl and rub about one-quarter of the spice paste into the meat. Cover and let marinate in the refrigerator for 30–40 minutes.

3 Heat the 4 tablespoons of oil in a medium heavy-bottom saucepan over medium heat, add the onions, and cook, stirring frequently, for 8–10 minutes, until lightly browned. Add the remaining spice paste and cook, stirring continuously, for 5–6 minutes. Add 2 tablespoons of the warm water and cook until it evaporates. Repeat with the other 2 tablespoons of warm water.

4 Add the marinated pork and cook over medium–high heat for 5–6 minutes, until the meat changes color. Add the salt, sugar, and 1 cup of warm water. Bring to a boil, then reduce the heat to low, cover, and simmer for 50–55 minutes.

5 Meanwhile, heat the 2 teaspoons of oil in a small saucepan over low heat. Add the sliced garlic and cook, stirring, until it begins to brown. Add the curry leaves and let sizzle for 15–20 seconds. Stir the garlic mixture into the vindaloo. Remove from the heat and serve immediately.

railroad pork & vegetables

ingredients

SERVES 4–6

3 tbsp ghee, vegetable oil,
    or peanut oil

1 large onion, finely chopped

4 green cardamom pods

3 cloves

1 cinnamon stick

1 tbsp garlic and ginger paste

2 tsp garam masala

$1/4$–$1/2$ tsp chili powder

$1/2$ tsp ground asafetida

2 tsp salt, or to taste

1 lb 5 oz/600 g lean ground
    pork

1 potato, scrubbed and cut
    into $1/4$-inch/5-mm dice

14 oz/400 g canned chopped
    tomatoes

$1/2$ cup water

1 bay leaf

1 large carrot, coarsely grated

pepper

method

1 Melt the ghee in a flameproof casserole or large skillet with a tight-fitting lid over medium heat. Add the onion and sauté, stirring occasionally, for 5–8 minutes, until golden brown. Add the cardamom pods, cloves, and cinnamon stick and continue sautéing, stirring, for 1 minute, or until you can smell the aromas.

2 Add the garlic and ginger paste, garam masala, chili powder, asafetida, and salt and stir for an additional minute. Add the pork and cook for 5 minutes, or until no longer pink, using a wooden spoon to break up the meat.

3 Add the potato, tomatoes, water, and bay leaf and bring to a boil, stirring. Reduce the heat to the lowest level, cover tightly, and simmer for 15 minutes. Stir in the carrot and simmer for an additional 5 minutes, or until the potato and carrot are tender. Taste and adjust the seasoning, adding salt and pepper if necessary, and serve.

pork with cinnamon & fenugreek

ingredients

SERVES 4

1 tsp ground coriander

1 tsp ground cumin

1 tsp chili powder

1 tbsp dried fenugreek leaves

1 tsp ground fenugreek

$^2/_3$ cup plain yogurt

1 lb/450 g diced pork
   tenderloin

4 tbsp ghee or vegetable oil

1 large onion, sliced

2-inch/5-cm piece fresh
   ginger, finely chopped

4 garlic cloves, finely
   chopped

1 cinnamon stick

6 green cardamom pods

6 whole cloves

2 bay leaves

$^3/_4$ cup water

salt

method

1 Mix the coriander, cumin, chili powder, dried fenugreek, ground fenugreek, and yogurt together in a small bowl. Place the pork in a large, shallow nonmetallic dish and add the spice mixture, turning well to coat. Cover with plastic wrap and let marinate in the refrigerator for 30 minutes.

2 Melt the ghee in a large heavy-bottom saucepan. Cook the onion over low heat, stirring occasionally, for 5 minutes, or until softened. Add the ginger, garlic, cinnamon stick, cardamom pods, cloves, and bay leaves and cook, stirring continuously, for 2 minutes, or until the spices give off their aroma. Add the meat with its marinade and the water, and season to taste with salt. Bring to a boil, reduce the heat, cover, and let simmer for 30 minutes.

3 Transfer the meat mixture to a preheated wok or large heavy-bottom skillet and cook over low heat, stirring continuously, until dry and tender. If necessary, sprinkle occasionally with a little water to prevent the mixture from sticking to the wok. Serve immediately.

pork with tamarind

ingredients

SERVES 6

2 oz/55 g dried tamarind,
    coarsely chopped

scant 2¹/₂ cups boiling water

2 fresh green chiles, seeded
    and coarsely chopped

2 onions, coarsely chopped

2 garlic cloves, coarsely
    chopped

1 lemongrass stalk, bulb end
    coarsely chopped

2 tbsp ghee or vegetable oil

1 tbsp ground coriander

1 tsp ground turmeric

1 tsp ground cardamom

1 tsp chili powder

1 tsp ginger paste

1 cinnamon stick

2 lb 4 oz/1 kg diced pork
    tenderloin

1 tbsp chopped fresh cilantro,
    plus extra sprigs to garnish

sliced fresh red chiles,
    to garnish

method

1 Place the dried tamarind in a small bowl, pour in the boiling water, and mix well. Let soak for 30 minutes.

2 Strain the soaking liquid into a clean bowl, pressing down the pulp with the back of a wooden spoon. Discard the pulp. Pour 1 tablespoon of the tamarind liquid into a food processor, add the green chiles, onions, garlic, and lemongrass, and process until smooth.

3 Heat the ghee in a large heavy-bottom saucepan. Add the chile-and-onion paste, coriander, turmeric, cardamom, chili powder, ginger paste, and cinnamon stick and cook, stirring, for 2 minutes, or until the spices give off their aroma.

4 Add the pork and cook, stirring constantly, until lightly browned and well coated in the spice mixture. Pour in the remaining tamarind liquid, bring to a boil, then reduce the heat, cover, and simmer for 30 minutes. Remove the lid from the saucepan and simmer for an additional 30 minutes, or until the pork is tender. Stir in the chopped cilantro and serve garnished with cilantro sprigs and sliced red chiles.

fish & seafood

The seas around India supply a wealth of fish and seafood and, hardly surprisingly, fish is on the menu every day in the south and west of the country. Indian cooks are used to preparing whatever looks tastiest and freshest in the day's catch, although pomfret and shrimp are particular favorites. This flexibility of approach makes it easy to adapt traditional recipes for varieties of fish more widely available in the West.

It is, perhaps, surprising how well fish and seafood go with all kinds of spices, whether in a fragrant mix with coconut milk, yogurt, or lime juice or in a sizzling hot chili sauce. Bengal is famous for its fish recipes and its use of pungent mustard oil—so be warned if you try a Bengali fish dish.

Fish is prepared in many different ways, so there is always something interesting on the menu. It may be pan-fried, deep-fried, or broiled, as fillets or in strips (often after coating with turmeric or other spices), stewed with mixed vegetables or beans, stir-fried, made into a flavorsome curry, cooked on skewers, or pickled and served cold. Shellfish dishes are just as varied and delicious, whether a spicy curry of jumbo shrimp or mussels cooked Goan-style in a delicate coconut sauce.

balti fish curry

ingredients

SERVES 4–6

2 lb/900 g thick whitefish
  fillets, rinsed and cut into
  large chunks
2 bay leaves, torn
$^2/_3$ cup ghee, vegetable oil,
  or peanut oil
2 large onions, chopped
$^1/_2$ tbsp salt
$^2/_3$ cup water
chopped fresh cilantro,
  to garnish
Indian bread, to serve

marinade

$^1/_2$ tbsp garlic and ginger
  paste
1 fresh green chile, seeded
  and chopped
1 tsp ground coriander
1 tsp ground cumin
$^1/_2$ tsp ground turmeric
$^1/_4$–$^1/_2$ tsp chili powder
1 tbsp water
salt

method

1 To make the marinade, mix the garlic and ginger paste, chile, coriander, cumin, turmeric, and chili powder together with salt to taste in a large bowl. Gradually stir in the water to form a thin paste. Add the fish chunks and smear with the marinade. Tuck the bay leaves underneath, cover, and let marinate in the refrigerator for at least 30 minutes, or up to 4 hours.

2 Remove the fish from the refrigerator 15 minutes in advance of cooking. Melt the ghee in a wok or large skillet over medium–high heat. Add the onions, sprinkle with the salt, and sauté, stirring frequently, for 8 minutes, or until they are very soft and golden.

3 Gently add the fish with its marinade and the bay leaves to the wok and stir in the water. Bring to a boil, then immediately reduce the heat and cook the fish for 4–5 minutes, spooning the sauce over the fish and carefully moving the chunks around, until they are cooked through and the flesh flakes easily. Garnish with cilantro and serve with Indian bread.

bengali-style fish

ingredients

SERVES 4–6

1 tsp ground turmeric

1 tsp salt

2 lb 4 oz/1 kg monkfish or
    cod fillet, skinned and
    cut into pieces

6 tbsp mustard oil

4 fresh green chiles

1 tsp finely chopped fresh
    ginger

1 tsp crushed garlic

2 onions, finely chopped

2 tomatoes, finely chopped

2 cups water

chopped fresh cilantro,
    to garnish

Indian bread, to serve

method

1 Mix the turmeric and salt together in a small bowl, then spoon the mixture over the fish pieces.

2 Heat the mustard oil in a large heavy-bottom skillet. Add the fish and cook until pale yellow. Remove the fish with a slotted spoon and set aside.

3 Place the chiles, ginger, garlic, onions, and tomatoes in a mortar and grind with a pestle to make a paste. Alternatively, place the ingredients in a food processor and process until smooth.

4 Transfer the spice paste to a clean skillet and dry-fry until golden brown.

5 Remove the skillet from the heat and place the fish pieces in the paste without breaking up the fish. Return the skillet to the heat, add the water, and cook over medium heat for 15–20 minutes. Transfer to a warmed serving dish, garnish with chopped cilantro, and serve with Indian bread.

goan-style seafood curry

ingredients

SERVES 4–6

3 tbsp vegetable oil or peanut
    oil

1 tbsp black mustard seeds

12 fresh or 1 tbsp dried curry
    leaves

6 shallots, finely chopped

1 garlic clove, crushed

1 tsp ground turmeric

$1/2$ tsp ground coriander

$1/4$–$1/2$ tsp chili powder

scant 3 cups coconut cream

1 lb 2 oz/500 g whitefish
    fillets, cut into large
    chunks

1 lb/450 g large raw shrimp,
    peeled and deveined

juice and finely grated rind of
    1 lime

salt

method

1 Heat the oil in a wok or large skillet over high heat. Add the mustard seeds and stir them around for about 1 minute, or until they pop. Stir in the curry leaves.

2 Add the shallots and garlic and stir for about 5 minutes, or until the shallots are golden. Stir in the turmeric, coriander, and chili powder and continue stirring for about 30 seconds.

3 Add the coconut cream. Bring to a boil, then reduce the heat to medium and stir for about 2 minutes.

4 Reduce the heat to low, add the fish, and simmer for 1 minute, spooning the sauce over the fish and very gently spooning it around. Add the shrimp and continue to simmer for an additional 4–5 minutes, until the fish flakes easily and the shrimp turn pink and curl.

5 Add half the lime juice, then taste and add more lime juice and salt to taste. Sprinkle with the lime rind and serve.

steamed fish with cilantro chutney

ingredients

SERVES 4

1 quantity cilantro chutney
(see page 198)
1 large fresh banana leaf
vegetable oil or peanut oil,
for brushing
4 whitefish fillets, such as
butterfish or sole, about
5 oz/140 g each
salt and pepper
lime or lemon wedges,
to serve

method

1 Prepare the cilantro chutney at least 2 hours in advance to let the flavors blend.

2 Meanwhile, cut the banana leaf into 4 squares large enough to fold comfortably around the fish to make tight pockets.

3 Working with one piece of leaf at a time, very lightly rub the bottom with oil. Put one of the fish fillets in the center of the oiled side, flesh-side up. Spread one-quarter of the cilantro chutney over the top and season to taste with salt and pepper.

4 Fold one side of the leaf over the fish, then fold the opposite side over. Turn the leaf so the folded edges are top and bottom. Fold the right-hand end of the leaf pocket into the center, then fold over the left-hand side. Trim the ends if the pocket becomes too bulky.

5 Use 2 wooden skewers to close the leaf pocket. Repeat with the remaining ingredients and banana leaf squares.

6 Place a steamer large enough to hold the pockets in a single layer over a pan of boiling water, without letting the water touch the fish. Add the fish, cover the pan, and steam for 15 minutes. Make sure the fish is cooked through and flakes easily.

7 Serve the fish pockets with lime or lemon wedges.

fish pakoras

ingredients

SERVES 4

$^1/_2$ tsp salt

2 tbsp lemon juice or distilled
  white vinegar

1 lb 9 oz/700 g skinless
  whitefish fillets, such as
  cod, halibut, or monkfish,
  rinsed, patted dry, and cut
  into large chunks

vegetable oil or peanut oil,
  for deep-frying

pepper

lemon wedges, to serve

batter

1 cup chickpea flour

seeds from 4 green
  cardamom pods

large pinch of ground
  turmeric

large pinch of baking soda

finely grated rind of 1 lemon

$^3/_4$ cup water

salt and pepper

method

1 Combine the salt, lemon juice, and pepper to taste and rub all over the fish chunks, then set aside in a nonmetallic bowl and let stand for 20–30 minutes.

2 Meanwhile, to make the batter, put the chickpea flour in a bowl and stir in the seeds from the cardamom pods, the turmeric, baking soda, lemon rind, and salt and pepper to taste. Make a well in the center and gradually stir in the water until a thin batter forms, similar in consistency to light cream.

3 Gently stir the pieces of fish into the batter, being careful to avoid breaking them up.

4 Heat enough oil for deep-frying in a wok, deep-fat fryer, or large heavy-bottom pan to 350°F/180°C, or until a cube of bread browns in 30 seconds. Remove the fish pieces from the batter and let the excess batter drip back into the bowl. Without overcrowding the pan, drop fish pieces in the hot oil and cook for about 2$^1/_2$–3 minutes, until golden brown.

5 Use a slotted spoon to remove the fish pieces from the oil and drain on crumpled paper towels. Continue until all the fish is cooked, then serve hot with the lemon wedges.

butterfish in chili yogurt

ingredients

SERVES 4

2 tbsp vegetable oil
   or peanut oil
1 large onion, sliced
1^1/$_2$-inch/4-cm piece fresh
   ginger, finely chopped
^{1}/$_2$ tsp salt
^{1}/$_4$ tsp ground turmeric
pinch of ground cinnamon
pinch of ground cloves
generous ^{3}/$_4$ cup plain yogurt
1 tbsp all-purpose flour
small pinch of chili powder
4 skinless butterfish fillets,
   about 5^1/$_2$ oz/150 g each,
   wiped dry
2 tbsp ghee, vegetable oil,
   or peanut oil
salt and pepper
2 fresh fat green chiles,
   seeded and finely
   chopped, to garnish

method

1 Heat the oil in a large skillet over medium–high heat. Add the onion and sauté, stirring, for 8 minutes, or until it is soft and dark golden brown. Add the ginger and stir around for an additional minute.

2 Stir in the salt, turmeric, cinnamon, and cloves and continue stirring for 30 seconds. Remove the pan from the heat and stir in the yogurt, a little at a time, beating constantly.

3 Transfer the yogurt mixture to a food processor or blender and process until a paste forms.

4 Season the flour with chili powder and salt and pepper to taste. Place it on a plate and lightly dust the fish fillets on both sides.

5 Melt the ghee in the wiped pan over medium–high heat. When it is bubbling, reduce the heat to medium and add the fish fillets in a single layer. Pan-fry for 2^1/$_2$ minutes, or until golden, then turn them over.

6 Continue cooking for an additional minute, then return the yogurt sauce to the pan and reheat, stirring. When the fillets flake easily and are cooked through and the sauce is hot, transfer to plates and sprinkle with the green chiles.

fish in tomato & chili sauce with fried onion

ingredients

SERVES 4

1 lb 9 oz/700 g tilapia fillets,
    cut into 2-inch/5-cm
    pieces
2 tbsp lemon juice
1 tsp salt, or to taste
1 tsp ground turmeric
4 tbsp sunflower oil or olive
    oil, plus extra for shallow-
    frying
2 tsp sugar
1 large onion, finely chopped
2 tsp ginger paste
2 tsp garlic paste
$1/2$ tsp ground fennel seeds
1 tsp ground coriander
$1/2$–1 tsp chili powder
6 oz/175 g canned chopped
    tomatoes
$1^1/4$ cups warm water
2–3 tbsp chopped fresh
    cilantro leaves
cooked basmati rice, to serve

method

1 Lay the fish on a plate and gently rub in the lemon juice, half the salt, and half the turmeric. Set aside for 15–20 minutes.

2 Pour enough oil to cover the bottom of a skillet to a depth of about $1/2$ inch/1 cm and place over medium–high heat. When the oil is hot, fry the fish in a single layer, until well browned on both sides. Drain on paper towels.

3 Heat the 4 tablespoons of oil in a medium saucepan over medium heat and add the sugar. Let it brown, watching it carefully because once it browns it will blacken quickly. Add the onion and cook for 5 minutes, until softened. Add the ginger and garlic pastes and cook for an additional 3–4 minutes.

4 Add the ground fennel seeds, coriander, chili powder, and the remaining turmeric. Cook for 1 minute, then add half the tomatoes. Cook until the tomato juice has evaporated, then add the remaining tomatoes. Cook, stirring, until the oil separates from the spice paste.

5 Pour in the warm water and add the remaining salt. Bring to a boil, then add the fish, stir gently, and reduce the heat to low. Cook, uncovered, for 5–6 minutes, then stir in half the cilantro leaves and remove from the heat. Sprinkle with the remaining cilantro and serve with cooked basmati rice.

fish korma

ingredients

SERVES 4

1 lb 9 oz/700 g tilapia fillets,
    cut into 2-inch/5-cm
    pieces
1 tbsp lemon juice
1 tsp salt
$1/2$ cup raw unsalted cashews
3 tbsp sunflower oil or olive oil
2-inch/5-cm piece cinnamon
    stick, halved
4 green cardamom pods,
    bruised
2 cloves
1 large onion, finely chopped
1–2 fresh green chiles,
    chopped (seeded if
    you like)
2 tsp ginger paste
2 tsp garlic paste
$2/3$ cup light cream
$1/4$ cup plain yogurt
$1/4$ tsp ground turmeric
$1/2$ tsp sugar
1 tbsp toasted slivered
    almonds, to garnish
Indian bread, to serve

method

1 Place the fish on a large plate and gently rub in the lemon juice and $1/2$ teaspoon of the salt. Set aside for 20 minutes. Put the cashews in a bowl, cover with boiling water, and let soak for 15 minutes.

2 Heat the oil in a wide shallow saucepan over low heat and add the cinnamon, cardamom, and cloves. Let them sizzle for 30–40 seconds.

3 Add the onion, chiles, ginger paste, and garlic paste. Increase the heat slightly and cook, stirring frequently, for 9–10 minutes, until the onion is very soft.

4 Meanwhile, drain the cashews and process them with the cream and yogurt.

5 Stir the turmeric into the onion mixture and add the processed ingredients, the remaining salt, and the sugar. Mix thoroughly and arrange the fish in the sauce in a single layer. Bring to a slow simmer, cover the pan, and cook for 5 minutes. Remove the lid and shake the pan gently from side to side. Spoon some of the sauce over the pieces of fish. Re-cover and cook for an additional 3–4 minutes.

6 Transfer to a serving dish and garnish with the slivered almonds. Serve with Indian bread.

goan fish curry

ingredients

SERVES 4

4 skinless salmon fillets,
about 7 oz/200 g each

1 tsp salt, or to taste

1 tbsp lemon juice

3 tbsp sunflower oil or olive oil

1 large onion, finely chopped

2 tsp garlic paste

2 tsp ginger paste

$1/2$ tsp ground turmeric

1 tsp ground coriander

$1/2$ tsp ground cumin

$1/2$–1 tsp chili powder

generous 1 cup canned
coconut milk

2–3 fresh green chiles, sliced
lengthwise (seeded if
you like)

2 tbsp cider vinegar or white
wine vinegar

2 tbsp chopped fresh cilantro
leaves

cooked basmati rice,
to serve

method

1 Cut each salmon fillet in half and lay on a flat surface in a single layer. Sprinkle with half the salt and the lemon juice and rub in gently. Cover and let marinate in the refrigerator for 15–20 minutes.

2 Heat the oil in a skillet over medium heat, add the onion, and cook, stirring frequently to ensure even coloring, for 8–9 minutes, until a pale golden color.

3 Add the garlic and ginger pastes and cook, stirring, for 1 minute, then add the turmeric, coriander, cumin, and chili powder and cook, stirring, for 1 minute. Add the coconut milk, chiles, and vinegar, then the remaining salt, stir well, and simmer, uncovered, for 6–8 minutes.

4 Add the fish and cook gently for 5–6 minutes. Stir in the fresh cilantro and remove from the heat. Serve immediately with cooked basmati rice.

fish tikka

ingredients

SERVES 4

pinch of saffron threads,
    pounded
1 tbsp hot milk
$1/3$ cup strained, whole-milk
    plain yogurt
1 tbsp garlic paste
1 tbsp ginger paste
1 tsp salt, or to taste
$1/2$ tsp granulated sugar
juice of $1/2$ lemon
$1/2$–1 tsp chili powder
$1/2$ tsp garam masala
1 tsp ground fennel seeds
2 tsp chickpea flour
1 lb 10 oz/750 g salmon
    fillets, skinned and cut
    into 2-inch/5-cm cubes
3 tbsp olive oil, plus extra for
    brushing
sliced tomatoes and
    cucumber, to garnish
lemon wedges, to serve

method

1 Soak the pounded saffron in the hot milk for 10 minutes.

2 Put all the remaining ingredients, except the fish and oil, in a bowl and beat with a fork or a wire whisk until smooth. Stir in the saffron and milk, mix well, and add the fish cubes. Using a metal spoon, mix gently, turning the fish around until fully coated with the marinade. Cover and let marinate in the refrigerator for 2 hours. Return to room temperature before cooking.

3 Preheat the broiler to high. Brush the rack generously with oil and 8 metal skewers lightly with oil. Line the broiler pan with a piece of foil.

4 Thread the fish cubes onto the prepared skewers, leaving a narrow gap between each piece. Arrange on the prepared rack and cook for 3 minutes. Brush half the 3 tablespoons of oil over the kabobs and cook for an additional minute. Turn over and brush any remaining marinade over the fish. Cook for 3 minutes. Brush the remaining oil over the fish and cook for an additional 2 minutes, or until the fish is lightly charred.

5 Remove from the heat and let rest for 5 minutes. Garnish with tomatoes and cucumber and serve with lemon wedges for squeezing over.

pickled mackerel

ingredients

SERVES 4

4 tbsp vegetable oil or peanut
    oil, plus extra for brushing
finely grated rind and juice
    of 1 lime
4 large mackerel fillets, about
    6 oz/175 g each
1¹/₂ tsp cumin seeds
1¹/₂ tsp black mustard seeds
1¹/₂ tsp nigella seeds
1¹/₂ tsp fennel seeds
1¹/₂ tsp coriander seeds
1¹/₂-inch/4-cm piece fresh
    ginger, very finely chopped
1¹/₂ garlic cloves, very finely
    chopped
3 shallots, very finely
    chopped
pinch of chili powder
salt and pepper
fresh red chiles, seeded
    and very finely sliced,
    to garnish
lime wedges, to serve

method

1 Mix together 2 tablespoons of the oil, the lime rind and juice, and salt and pepper to taste in a nonmetallic bowl that will hold the mackerel fillets in a single layer. Add the mackerel fillets and use your hands to cover them in the marinade, then set aside for at least 10 minutes, or cover and chill for up to 4 hours.

2 Meanwhile, preheat the broiler to high and lightly brush the broiler rack with oil.

3 Remove the mackerel from the refrigerator 15 minutes in advance of cooking. Put the mackerel on the broiler rack, skin-side down, and broil for 6 minutes, or until the flesh is cooked through when pierced with the tip of a knife and flakes easily.

4 Meanwhile, heat the remaining oil in a wok or large skillet over medium–high heat. Add the cumin seeds, black mustard seeds, nigella seeds, fennel seeds, and coriander seeds and stir around until the mustard seeds start to jump and the coriander and cumin seeds just start to brown. Immediately remove the pan from the heat, then stir in the ginger, garlic, shallots, and chili powder and continue stirring for 1 minute.

5 Transfer the mackerel fillets to plates and spoon over the spice mixture. Garnish with red chile slices and serve with lime wedges for squeezing over.

goan shrimp curry with hard-cooked eggs

ingredients

SERVES 4

4 tbsp sunflower oil or olive oil

1 large onion, finely chopped

2 tsp ginger paste

2 tsp garlic paste

2 tsp ground coriander

$1/2$ tsp ground fennel

$1/2$ tsp ground turmeric

$1/2$–1 tsp chili powder

$1/2$ tsp pepper

2–3 tbsp water

$4^1/2$ oz/125 g canned
   chopped tomatoes

scant 1 cup coconut milk

1 tsp salt, or to taste

4 hard-cooked eggs

1 lb 9 oz/700 g cooked
   peeled jumbo shrimp

juice of 1 lime

2–3 tbsp chopped fresh
   cilantro leaves

cooked basmati rice, to serve

method

1 Heat the oil in a medium saucepan over medium–high heat and add the onion. Cook until the onion is softened but not browned. Add the ginger paste and garlic paste and cook for 2–3 minutes.

2 In a small bowl, combine the coriander, fennel, turmeric, chili powder, and pepper. Add the water and make a paste. Reduce the heat to medium, add the paste to the onion mixture, and cook for 1–2 minutes. Reduce the heat to low and continue to cook for 3–4 minutes.

3 Add half the tomatoes and cook for 2–3 minutes. Add the remaining tomatoes and cook for an additional 2–3 minutes.

4 Add the coconut milk and salt, bring to a slow simmer, and cook, uncovered, for 6–8 minutes, stirring frequently.

5 Meanwhile, shell the eggs and, using a sharp knife, make 4 slits lengthwise on each egg without cutting through. Add the eggs to the pan along with the shrimp. Increase the heat slightly and cook for 6–8 minutes.

6 Stir in the lime juice and half the cilantro. Remove from the heat and transfer the curry to a serving dish. Garnish with the remaining cilantro and serve with cooked basmati rice.

shrimp in coconut milk

ingredients

SERVES 4

1 lb 2 oz/500 g raw jumbo
  shrimp

4 onions

4 tbsp ghee or vegetable oil

1 tsp garam masala

1 tsp ground turmeric

1 cinnamon stick

2 green cardamom pods,
  bruised

$1/2$ tsp chili powder

2 whole cloves

2 bay leaves

$1^3/4$ cups coconut milk

1 tsp sugar

salt

pilaf rice, to serve

method

1 Shell and devein the jumbo shrimp, then set aside until required. Finely chop 2 of the onions and grate the other 2. Heat the ghee in a large heavy-bottom skillet. Add the garam masala and cook over low heat, stirring constantly, for 1 minute, or until its aroma is released. Add the chopped onions and cook, stirring occasionally, for 10 minutes, or until golden.

2 Stir in the grated onions, turmeric, cinnamon, cardamom pods, chili powder, cloves, and bay leaves and cook, stirring constantly, for 5 minutes. Stir in half the coconut milk and the sugar and season to taste with salt. Add the shrimp and cook, stirring frequently for 8 minutes, or until they have changed color.

3 Stir in the remaining coconut milk and bring to a boil. Taste and adjust the seasoning, if necessary, and serve immediately with pilaf rice.

shrimp biryani

ingredients

SERVES 8

1 tsp saffron strands

4 tbsp lukewarm water

2 shallots, coarsely chopped

3 garlic cloves, crushed

1-inch/2.5-cm piece fresh
ginger, chopped

2 tsp coriander seeds

$^1/_2$ tsp black peppercorns

2 cloves

seeds from 2 green
cardamom pods

1-inch/2.5-cm piece
cinnamon stick

1 tsp ground turmeric

1 fresh green chile, chopped

$^1/_2$ tsp salt

2 tbsp ghee

1 tsp black mustard seeds

1 lb 2 oz/500 g raw jumbo
shrimp in their shells, or
14 oz/400 g raw shrimp,
peeled and deveined

$1^1/_4$ cups coconut milk

$1^1/_4$ cups lowfat plain yogurt

cooked basmati rice, to serve

to garnish

toasted slivered almonds

1 scallion, sliced

fresh cilantro sprigs

method

1 Soak the saffron in the lukewarm water for 10 minutes. Put the shallots, garlic, ginger, coriander seeds, peppercorns, cloves, cardamom seeds, cinnamon stick, turmeric, chile, and salt into a spice grinder or mortar and grind to a paste.

2 Heat the ghee in a saucepan and add the mustard seeds. When they start to pop, add the shrimp and stir over a high heat for 1 minute. Stir in the spice mix, then the coconut milk and yogurt. Simmer for 20 minutes.

3 Spoon the shrimp mixture into warmed serving dishes. Top with the cooked basmati rice and drizzle over the saffron water. Serve garnished with the almonds, scallion, and cilantro sprigs.

tandoori shrimp

ingredients

SERVES 4

4 tbsp plain yogurt

2 fresh green chiles, seeded
and chopped

$1/2$ tbsp garlic and ginger
paste

seeds from 4 green
cardamom pods

2 tsp ground cumin

1 tsp tomato paste

$1/4$ tsp ground turmeric

$1/4$ tsp salt

pinch of chili powder, ideally
Kashmiri chili powder

24 raw jumbo shrimp, thawed
if frozen, peeled, deveined,
and tails left intact

oil, for greasing

lemon or lime wedges,
to serve

method

1 Put the yogurt, chiles, and garlic and ginger paste in a small food processor or spice grinder and process to a paste. Alternatively use a pestle and mortar. Transfer the paste to a large nonmetallic bowl and stir in the cardamom seeds, cumin, tomato paste, turmeric, salt, and chili powder.

2 Add the shrimp to the bowl and use your hands to make sure they are coated with the yogurt marinade. Cover the bowl with plastic wrap and chill for at least 30 minutes, or up to 4 hours.

3 When you are ready to cook, heat a large grill pan or skillet over high heat until a few drops of water "dance" when they hit the surface. Use crumpled paper towels or a pastry brush to grease the hot pan very lightly with oil.

4 Use tongs to lift the shrimp out of the marinade, letting the excess drip back into the bowl, then place the shrimp on the pan and cook for 2 minutes. Flip the shrimp over and cook for an additional 1–2 minutes, until they turn pink, curl, and are opaque all the way through when you cut one. Serve the shrimp immediately with lemon or lime wedges for squeezing over.

shrimp & pineapple tikka

ingredients

SERVES 4

1 tsp cumin seeds

1 tsp coriander seeds

$1/2$ tsp fennel seeds

$1/2$ tsp yellow mustard seeds

$1/4$ tsp fenugreek seeds

$1/4$ tsp nigella seeds

pinch of chili powder

2 tbsp lemon or pineapple
    juice

12 raw jumbo shrimp, peeled,
    deveined, and tails
    left intact

12 bite-size wedges of fresh
    or well-drained canned
    pineapple

salt

chopped fresh cilantro,
    to garnish

method

1 If you are using wooden skewers for this rather than metal ones, place 4 skewers upright in a tall glass of water to soak for 20 minutes so they do not burn under the broiler.

2 Dry-roast the cumin, coriander, fennel, mustard, fenugreek, and nigella seeds in a hot skillet over high heat, stirring them around constantly, until you can smell the aroma of the spices. Immediately turn the spices out of the pan so they do not burn.

3 Put the spices in a spice grinder or mortar, add the chili powder and salt to taste, and grind to a fine powder. Transfer to a nonmetallic bowl and stir in the lemon juice.

4 Add the shrimp to the bowl and stir them around so they are well coated, then set aside to marinate for 10 minutes. Meanwhile, preheat the broiler to high.

5 Thread 3 shrimp and 3 pineapple wedges alternately onto each wooden or metal skewer. Broil about 4 inches/10 cm from the heat for 2 minutes on each side, brushing with any leftover marinade, until the shrimp turn pink and are cooked through.

6 Serve the shrimp and pineapple wedges on the skewers on a plate with plenty of cilantro sprinkled over.

shrimp in coconut milk with chiles & curry leaves

ingredients

SERVES 4

4 tbsp sunflower oil or olive oil

1/2 tsp black or brown
    mustard seeds

1/2 tsp fenugreek seeds

1 large onion, finely chopped

2 tsp garlic paste

2 tsp ginger paste

1–2 fresh green chiles,
    chopped (seeded if
    you like)

1 tbsp ground coriander

1/2 tsp ground turmeric

1/2 tsp chili powder

1 tsp salt, or to taste

generous 1 cup canned
    coconut milk

1 lb/450 g cooked, peeled
    jumbo shrimp, thawed
    and drained if frozen

1 tbsp tamarind juice or
    juice of 1/2 lime

1/2 tsp crushed black pepper

10–12 fresh or dried curry
    leaves

method

1 Heat 3 tablespoons of the oil in a medium saucepan over medium–high heat. When hot, but not smoking, add the mustard seeds, followed by the fenugreek seeds and the onion. Cook, stirring frequently, for 5–6 minutes, until the onion is softened but not browned. Add the garlic and ginger pastes and the chiles and cook, stirring frequently, for an additional 5–6 minutes, until the onion is a light golden color.

2 Add the coriander, turmeric, and chili powder and cook, stirring, for 1 minute. Add the salt and coconut milk, followed by the shrimp and tamarind juice. Bring to a slow simmer and cook, stirring occasionally, for 3–4 minutes.

3 Meanwhile, heat the remaining oil in a very small saucepan over medium heat. Add the pepper and curry leaves. Turn off the heat and let sizzle for 20–25 seconds, then fold the aromatic oil into the shrimp mixture. Remove from the heat and serve immediately.

mussels with mustard seeds & shallots

ingredients

SERVES 4

4 lb 8 oz/2 kg mussels, scrubbed and debearded

3 tbsp vegetable oil or peanut oil

$1/2$ tbsp black mustard seeds

8 shallots, chopped

2 garlic cloves, crushed

2 tbsp distilled white vinegar

4 small fresh red chiles

$1^1/4$ cups coconut cream

10 fresh or 1 tbsp dried curry leaves

$1/2$ tsp ground turmeric

$1/4$–$1/2$ tsp chili powder

salt

method

1 Discard any mussels with broken shells and any that refuse to close when tapped with a knife. Set aside.

2 Heat the oil in a wok or large skillet over medium–high heat. Add the mustard seeds and stir them around for 1 minute, or until they start to pop.

3 Add the shallots and garlic and cook, stirring frequently, for 3 minutes, or until they start to brown. Stir in the vinegar, whole chiles, coconut cream, curry leaves, turmeric, chili powder, and a pinch of salt and bring to a boil, stirring.

4 Reduce the heat to very low. Add the mussels, cover the wok, and let the mussels simmer, shaking the wok frequently, for 3–4 minutes, or until they are all open. Discard any mussels that remain closed. Ladle the mussels into deep bowls, then taste the broth and add extra salt, if necessary. Spoon over the mussels and serve.

mussels in coconut sauce

ingredients

SERVES 4

2 lb 4 oz/1 kg mussels,
  scrubbed and debearded

3 tbsp ghee or vegetable oil

1 onion, finely chopped

1 tsp garlic paste

1 tsp ginger paste

1 tsp ground cumin

1 tsp ground coriander

$^1/_2$ tsp ground turmeric

pinch of salt

$2^1/_2$ cups canned coconut
  milk

chopped fresh cilantro,
  to garnish

method

1 Discard any mussels with broken shells and any that refuse to close when tapped with a knife. Set aside.

2 Heat the ghee in a large heavy-bottom skillet. Add the onion and cook over low heat, stirring occasionally, for 10 minutes, or until golden.

3 Add the garlic and ginger pastes and cook, stirring constantly, for 2 minutes. Add the cumin, ground coriander, turmeric, and salt and cook, stirring constantly, for an additional 2 minutes. Stir in the coconut milk and bring to a boil.

4 Add the mussels, cover, and cook for 5 minutes, or until the mussels have opened. Discard any mussels that remain closed. Transfer the mussels, with the coconut sauce, to a large warmed serving dish. Sprinkle with chopped cilantro and serve immediately.

vegetables & legumes

Many Indians are vegetarian either because of religious belief or as a result of poverty, so the imaginative diversity of dishes based on vegetables and legumes is breathtaking. Indian cooks treat vegetables with great respect—not surprising in a country that boasts 18 different varieties of spinach. The keynote of vegetable dishes is contrasting flavors, so hot spices are matched with cooling yogurt or sour tamarind, and savory greens with sweet nuts or fruit. Virtually all vegetables familiar to western cooks are at home in the Indian kitchen, too—onions, potatoes, eggplants, bell peppers, tomatoes, cauliflower, okra, spinach, peas, and green beans—so as well as a huge choice of main-course vegetarian dishes, there is always an ideal side dish to choose.

Dried beans, chickpeas, lentils, and split peas are very nutritious and have a natural affinity with herbs and spices. They may be cooked whole or pureed and made into dhal—virtually every region of India has its own dhal specialty. They can also, of course, be combined with each other and/or vegetables.

Dried beans need to be soaked in cold water for several hours before cooking. However, for your convenience, most of the recipes in this book use canned beans, which are presoaked and cooked and, therefore, considerably reduce the overall cooking time.

vegetable korma

ingredients

SERVES 4

$^1/_2$ cup raw cashews

$^3/_4$ cup boiling water

good pinch of saffron threads,
    pounded

2 tbsp hot milk

1 head of cauliflower, divided
    into $^1/_2$-inch/1-cm florets

4 oz/115 g green beans, cut
    into 1-inch/2.5-cm lengths

2 carrots, cut into
    1-inch/2.5-cm sticks

4 tbsp sunflower oil or olive oil

1 large onion, finely chopped

2 tsp ginger paste

1–2 fresh green chiles,
    chopped (seeded if
    you like)

2 tsp ground coriander

$^1/_2$ tsp ground turmeric

6 tbsp warm water

1$^3/_4$ cups vegetable stock

$^1/_2$ tsp salt, or to taste

9 oz/250 g young, waxy
    potatoes, boiled in their
    skins, cooled, and halved

2 tbsp light cream

2 tsp ghee or butter

1 tsp garam masala

$^1/_4$ tsp grated nutmeg

method

1 Soak the cashews in the boiling water in a heatproof bowl for 20 minutes. Meanwhile, soak the pounded saffron in the hot milk.

2 Blanch the vegetables in a saucepan of boiling salted water, then drain and immediately plunge in cold water. The cauliflower and green beans should each be blanched for 3 minutes; the carrots will need 4 minutes.

3 Heat the oil in a medium heavy-bottom saucepan over medium heat. Add the onion, ginger paste, and chiles and cook, stirring frequently, for 5–6 minutes, until the onion is softened. Add the coriander and turmeric and cook, stirring, for 1 minute. Add half the warm water and cook for 2–3 minutes. Repeat this process with the remaining warm water, then cook, stirring frequently, for 2–3 minutes, or until the oil separates from the spice paste.

4 Add the stock, saffron and milk mixture, and salt, and bring to a boil. Drain the vegetables, add to the saucepan with the potatoes, and return to a boil. Reduce the heat to low and simmer for 2–3 minutes.

5 Meanwhile, put the cashews and their soaking water in a food processor and process until well blended. Add to the korma, then stir in the cream. Reduce the heat to very low.

6 Melt the ghee in a small saucepan over low heat. Add the garam masala and nutmeg and sizzle gently for 20–25 seconds. Fold the spiced butter into the korma. Remove from the heat and serve.

cauliflower, eggplant & green bean korma

ingredients

SERVES 4–6

generous $^1/_2$ cup cashews

$1^1/_2$ tbsp garlic and ginger paste

scant 1 cup water

4 tbsp ghee, vegetable oil, or peanut oil

1 large onion, chopped

5 green cardamom pods, bruised

1 cinnamon stick, broken in half

$^1/_4$ tsp ground turmeric

generous 1 cup heavy cream

5 oz/140 g new potatoes, scrubbed and chopped into $^1/_2$-inch/1-cm pieces

$1^1/_2$ cups cauliflower florets

$^1/_2$ tsp garam masala

5 oz/140 g eggplant, chopped into 1-inch/2.5-cm chunks

5 oz/140 g green beans, chopped into 1-inch/2.5-cm lengths

salt and pepper

chopped fresh mint, to garnish

method

1 Heat a large flameproof casserole over high heat. Add the cashews and stir them until they start to brown, then immediately turn them out of the casserole.

2 Put the nuts in a spice grinder with the garlic and ginger paste and 1 tablespoon of the water and process to a coarse paste.

3 Melt half the ghee in the casserole over medium–high heat. Add the onion and sauté for 5–8 minutes, until golden brown.

4 Add the nut paste and stir for 5 minutes. Stir in the cardamom pods, cinnamon stick, and turmeric.

5 Add the cream and the remaining water and bring to a boil, stirring. Reduce the heat to very low, cover, and simmer for 5 minutes.

6 Add the potatoes, cauliflower, and garam masala and simmer, covered, for 5 minutes. Stir in the eggplant and green beans and simmer for an additional 5 minutes, or until all the vegetables are tender. Check the sauce occasionally to make sure it isn't sticking, and stir in a little water if needed.

7 Taste and add seasoning, if necessary. Sprinkle with the mint and serve.

cumin-scented eggplant & potato curry

ingredients

SERVES 4

1 large eggplant, about
    12 oz/350 g
8 oz/225 g potatoes, boiled in
    their skins and cooled
3 tbsp sunflower oil or olive oil
$^1/_2$ tsp black mustard seeds
$^1/_2$ tsp nigella seeds
$^1/_2$ tsp fennel seeds
1 onion, finely chopped
1-inch/2.5-cm piece fresh
    ginger, grated
2 fresh green chiles, chopped
    (seeded if you like)
$^1/_2$ tsp ground cumin
1 tsp ground coriander
1 tsp ground turmeric
$^1/_2$ tsp chili powder
1 tbsp tomato paste
scant 2 cups warm water
1 tsp salt, or to taste
$^1/_2$ tsp garam masala
2 tbsp chopped fresh cilantro
    leaves
Indian bread, to serve

method

1 Quarter the eggplant lengthwise and cut the stem end of each quarter into 2-inch/5-cm pieces. Halve the remaining part of the quarter and cut into 2-inch/5-cm pieces. Soak the eggplant pieces in cold water.

2 Peel the potatoes and cut into 2-inch/5-cm cubes. Set aside. Heat the oil in a large saucepan over medium heat. When hot, add the mustard seeds and, as soon as they start popping, add the nigella seeds and fennel seeds.

3 Add the onion, ginger, and chiles and cook for 7–8 minutes, until the mixture begins to brown.

4 Add the cumin, coriander, turmeric, and chili powder. Cook for about 1 minute, then add the tomato paste. Cook for an additional minute, then pour in the warm water and add the salt and drained eggplant. Bring to a boil and cook over medium heat for 8–10 minutes, stirring frequently to make sure that the eggplant cooks evenly. At the start of cooking, the eggplant will float, but once it soaks up the liquid it will sink quickly. As soon as the eggplant sinks, add the potatoes and cook for an additional 2–3 minutes, stirring.

5 Stir in the garam masala and chopped cilantro and remove from the heat. Serve with Indian bread.

pumpkin curry

ingredients

SERVES 4

$^2/_3$ cup vegetable oil

2 onions, sliced

$^1/_2$ tsp white cumin seeds

1 lb/450 g pumpkin, cubed

1 tsp amchoor (dried mango
   powder)

1 tsp fresh ginger, chopped

1 tsp crushed garlic

1 tsp chile flakes

$^1/_2$ tsp salt

1$^1/_4$ cups water

chapatis, to serve

method

1 Heat the oil in a large heavy-bottom skillet. Add the onions and cumin seeds and cook, stirring occasionally, for 5–6 minutes, until a golden brown color.

2 Add the pumpkin to the skillet and stir-fry for 3–5 minutes over low heat.

3 Mix the amchoor, ginger, garlic, chile flakes, and salt together in a bowl. Add to the onion-and-pumpkin mixture in the pan and stir well.

4 Add the water, cover, and cook over low heat for 10–15 minutes, stirring occasionally. Transfer the curry to warmed serving dishes and serve hot with chapatis.

cauliflower & sweet potato curry

ingredients

SERVES 4

4 tbsp ghee or vegetable oil

2 onions, finely chopped

1 tsp Bengali five-spice mix

1 head of cauliflower, broken
  into florets

12 oz/350 g sweet potatoes,
  diced

2 fresh green chiles, seeded
  and finely chopped

1 tsp ginger paste

2 tsp paprika

$1^1/_2$ tsp ground cumin

1 tsp ground turmeric

$^1/_2$ tsp chili powder

3 tomatoes, quartered

2 cups fresh or frozen peas

3 tbsp plain yogurt

1 cup vegetable stock or
  water

1 tsp garam masala

salt

fresh cilantro sprigs,
  to garnish

method

1 Heat the ghee in a large heavy-bottom skillet. Add the onions and Bengali five-spice mix and cook over low heat, stirring frequently, for 10 minutes, or until the onions are golden. Add the cauliflower, sweet potatoes, and chiles and cook, stirring frequently, for 3 minutes.

2 Stir in the ginger paste, paprika, cumin, turmeric, and chili powder and cook, stirring constantly, for 3 minutes. Add the tomatoes and peas and stir in the yogurt and stock. Season with salt to taste, cover, and let simmer for 20 minutes, or until the vegetables are tender.

3 Sprinkle over the garam masala and transfer to a warmed serving dish. Garnish with cilantro sprigs and serve immediately.

mushroom bhaji

ingredients

SERVES 4

10 oz/280 g button mushrooms

4 tbsp sunflower oil or olive oil

1 onion, finely chopped

1 fresh green chile, finely
    chopped (seeded if
    you like)

2 tsp garlic paste

1 tsp ground cumin

1 tsp ground coriander

$^1/_2$ tsp chili powder

$^1/_2$ tsp salt, or to taste

1 tbsp tomato paste

3 tbsp water

1 tbsp snipped fresh chives,
    to garnish

method

1 Wipe the mushrooms with damp paper towels and slice thickly.

2 Heat the oil in a medium saucepan over medium heat. Add the onion and chile and cook, stirring, for 5–6 minutes, until the onion is softened but not browned. Add the garlic paste and cook, stirring, for 2 minutes.

3 Add the cumin, coriander, and chili powder and cook, stirring, for 1 minute. Add the mushrooms, salt, and tomato paste and stir until all the ingredients are blended.

4 Sprinkle the water evenly over the mushrooms and reduce the heat to low. Cover and cook for 5 minutes, stir, then cook for an additional 5 minutes. The sauce should have thickened, but if it appears runny, cook, uncovered, for 3–4 minutes, or until you achieve the desired consistency.

5 Transfer to a serving dish, sprinkle the chives on top, and serve immediately.

okra stir-fried with onions

ingredients

SERVES 4

10 oz/280 g okra

1 small red bell pepper

1 onion

2 tbsp sunflower oil or olive oil

1 tsp black or brown mustard
seeds

1/2 tsp cumin seeds

3 large garlic cloves, lightly
crushed, then chopped

1/2 tsp chili powder

1/2 tsp salt, or to taste

1/2 tsp garam masala

cooked basmati rice,
to serve

method

1 Scrub each okra gently, rinse well in cold running water, then slice off the hard head. Halve diagonally and set aside.

2 Remove the seeds and core from the red bell pepper and cut into 1 1/2-inch/4-cm strips. Halve the onion lengthwise and cut into 1/4 inch/5 mm thick slices.

3 Heat the oil in a heavy-bottom skillet or wok over medium heat. When hot, but not smoking, add the mustard seeds, followed by the cumin seeds. Remove from the heat and add the garlic. Return to low heat and cook the garlic gently, stirring, for 1 minute, or until lightly browned.

4 Add the okra, red bell pepper, and onion, increase the heat to medium–high, and stir-fry for 2 minutes. Add the chili powder and salt and stir-fry for an additional 3 minutes. Add the garam masala and stir-fry for 1 minute. Remove from the heat and serve immediately with cooked basmati rice.

spiced balti cabbage

ingredients

SERVES 4

2 tbsp vegetable oil
or peanut oil

$1/2$ tbsp cumin seeds

2 large garlic cloves, crushed

1 large onion, thinly sliced

1 lb 5 oz/600 g savoy
cabbage, cored and thinly
sliced

$2/3$ cup balti sauce
(see page 66)

$1/4$ tsp garam masala

salt

chopped fresh cilantro,
to garnish

method

1 Heat the oil in a wok or large skillet over medium–high heat. Add the cumin seeds and stir for about 80 seconds, until they start to brown.

2 Immediately stir in the garlic and onion and sauté, stirring frequently, for 5–8 minutes, until golden.

3 Add the cabbage to the pan and stir for 2 minutes, or until it starts to wilt. Stir in the balti sauce and bring to a boil, stirring. Reduce the heat a little and simmer for 3–5 minutes, until the cabbage is tender.

4 Stir in the garam masala and add salt to taste. Sprinkle with the cilantro and serve.

garlic & chile-flavored potatoes with cauliflower

ingredients

SERVES 4

12 oz/350 g young, waxy potatoes

1 head of cauliflower

2 tbsp sunflower oil or olive oil

1 tsp black or brown mustard seeds

1 tsp cumin seeds

5 large garlic cloves, lightly crushed, then chopped

1–2 fresh green chiles, finely chopped (seeded if you like)

$1/2$ tsp ground turmeric

$1/2$ tsp salt, or to taste

2 tbsp chopped fresh cilantro leaves

method

1 Cook the potatoes in their skins in a saucepan of boiling water for 20 minutes, or until tender. Drain, then soak in cold water for 30 minutes. Peel them, if you like, then halve or quarter according to their size—they should be only slightly bigger than the size of the cauliflower florets.

2 Meanwhile, divide the cauliflower into about $1/2$-inch/1-cm florets and blanch in a large saucepan of boiling salted water for 3 minutes. Drain and plunge into iced water to prevent additional cooking, then drain again.

3 Heat the oil in a medium saucepan over medium heat. When hot, but not smoking, add the mustard seeds, then the cumin seeds. Remove from the heat and add the garlic and chiles. Return to a low heat and cook, stirring, until the garlic has a light brown tinge.

4 Stir in the turmeric, followed by the cauliflower and the potatoes. Add the salt, increase the heat slightly, and cook, stirring, until the vegetables are well blended with the spices and heated through.

5 Stir in the cilantro, remove from the heat, and serve immediately.

potatoes with spiced spinach

ingredients

SERVES 4

12 oz/350 g young, waxy
   potatoes
9 oz/250 g spinach leaves,
   defrosted if frozen
3 tbsp sunflower oil or olive oil
1 large onion, finely sliced
1 fresh green chile, finely
   chopped (seeded if
   you like)
2 tsp garlic paste
2 tsp ginger paste
1 tsp ground coriander
$1/2$ tsp ground cumin
$1/2$ tsp chili powder
$1/2$ tsp ground turmeric
7 oz/200 g canned chopped
   tomatoes
$1/2$ tsp granulated sugar
1 tsp salt, or to taste
3 tbsp light cream

method

1 Cook the potatoes in their skins in a saucepan of boiling water for 20 minutes, or until tender. Drain, then soak in cold water for 30 minutes. Peel them, if you like, then halve or quarter.

2 Meanwhile, cook the spinach in a large saucepan of boiling water for 2 minutes, then drain. Transfer to a food processor and blend to a paste.

3 Heat 2 tablespoons of the oil in a medium saucepan over medium heat. Add the onion and cook, stirring, for 10–12 minutes, until browned, reducing the heat to low for the last 2–3 minutes. Remove from the heat and remove the excess oil from the onion by pressing it against the side of the saucepan with a wooden spoon. Drain on paper towels.

4 Return the pan to the heat, add the remaining oil, and heat. Add the chile and garlic and ginger pastes and cook over low heat, stirring, for 2–3 minutes. Add the coriander, cumin, chili powder, and turmeric and cook, stirring, for 1 minute. Add the tomatoes, increase the heat to medium, and add the sugar. Cook, stirring, for 5–6 minutes.

5 Add the potatoes, spinach, salt, and reserved onion and cook, stirring, for 2–3 minutes. Stir in the cream and cook for 1 minute. Remove from the heat and serve.

garden peas & paneer in chili-tomato sauce

ingredients

SERVES 4

4 tbsp sunflower oil or olive oil

9 oz/250 g paneer, cut into
 1-inch/2.5-cm cubes

4 green cardamom pods,
 bruised

2 bay leaves

1 onion, finely chopped

2 tsp garlic paste

2 tsp ginger paste

2 tsp ground coriander

$1/2$ tsp ground turmeric

$1/2$–1 tsp chili powder

$5^1/2$ oz/150 g canned
 chopped tomatoes

scant 2 cups warm water,
 plus 2 tbsp

1 tsp salt, or to taste

$1^1/4$ cups frozen peas

$1/2$ tsp garam masala

2 tbsp light cream

2 tbsp chopped fresh cilantro
 leaves

method

1 Heat 2 tablespoons of the oil in a medium nonstick saucepan over medium heat. Add the paneer and cook, stirring frequently, for 3–4 minutes, or until evenly browned. Paneer tends to splatter in hot oil, so be careful. Remove and drain on paper towels.

2 Add the remaining oil to the saucepan and reduce the heat to low. Add the cardamom pods and bay leaves and let sizzle gently for 20–25 seconds. Add the onion, increase the heat to medium, and cook, stirring frequently, for 4–5 minutes, until the onion is softened. Add the garlic and ginger pastes and cook, stirring frequently, for an additional 3–4 minutes, until the onion is a pale golden color.

3 Add the coriander, turmeric, and chili powder and cook, stirring, for 1 minute. Add the tomatoes and cook, stirring, for 4–5 minutes. Add the 2 tablespoons of warm water and cook, stirring, for 3 minutes, or until the oil separates from the spice paste.

4 Add the scant 2 cups of warm water and salt. Bring to a boil, then reduce the heat to low and simmer, uncovered, for 7–8 minutes.

5 Add the paneer and peas and simmer for 5 minutes. Stir in the garam masala, cream, and fresh cilantro and remove from the heat.

chickpeas in coconut milk

ingredients

SERVES 4

generous 1 cup water

10 oz/280 g potatoes, cut into
    1/2-inch/1-cm cubes

14 oz/400 g canned chickpeas,
    drained and well rinsed

generous 1 cup canned
    coconut milk

1 tsp salt, or to taste

2 tbsp sunflower oil or olive oil

4 large garlic cloves, finely
    chopped or crushed

2 tsp ground coriander

1/2 tsp ground turmeric

1/2–1 tsp chili powder

juice of 1/2 lemon

Indian bread, to serve

method

1 Pour the water into a medium saucepan and add the potatoes. Bring to a boil, then reduce the heat to low and cook, covered, for 6–7 minutes, until the potatoes are al dente. Add the chickpeas and cook, uncovered, for 3–4 minutes, until the potatoes are tender. Add the coconut milk and salt and bring to a slow simmer.

2 Meanwhile, heat the oil in a small saucepan over low heat. Add the garlic and cook, stirring frequently, until it begins to brown. Add the coriander, turmeric, and chili powder and cook, stirring, for 25–30 seconds.

3 Fold the aromatic oil into the chickpea mixture. Stir in the lemon juice and remove from the heat. Serve immediately with Indian bread.

chickpeas with spiced tomatoes

ingredients

SERVES 4

6 tbsp vegetable oil
   or peanut oil
2 tsp cumin seeds
3 large onions, finely chopped
2 tsp garlic and ginger paste
2 small fresh green chiles,
   seeded and thinly sliced
$1^1/_2$ tsp amchoor
   (dried mango powder)
$1^1/_2$ tsp garam masala
$^3/_4$ tsp ground asafetida
$^1/_2$ tsp ground turmeric
$^1/_4$–1 tsp chili powder
3 large firm tomatoes, about
   1 lb/450 g, grated
1 lb 12 oz/800 g canned
   chickpeas, rinsed and
   drained
6 tbsp water
$10^1/_2$ oz/300 g fresh spinach
   leaves, rinsed
$^1/_2$ tsp salt, or to taste

method

1 Heat the oil in a wok or large skillet over medium–high heat. Add the cumin seeds and stir around for 30 seconds, or until they brown and crackle, watching carefully because they can burn quickly.

2 Immediately stir in the onions, garlic and ginger paste, and chiles and sauté, stirring frequently, for 5–8 minutes, until the onions are golden.

3 Stir in the amchoor, garam masala, asafetida, turmeric, and chili powder. Add the tomatoes to the pan, stir them around, and continue cooking, stirring frequently, until the sauce blends together and starts to brown slightly.

4 Stir in the chickpeas and water and bring to a boil. Reduce the heat to very low and use a wooden spoon or a potato masher to mash about one-quarter of the chickpeas, leaving the remainder whole.

5 Add the spinach to the pan with just the water clinging to the leaves and stir around until it wilts and is cooked. Stir in the salt, then taste and adjust the seasoning, adding more salt if necessary.

black-eyed peas & mushrooms

ingredients

SERVES 4

1 onion, coarsely chopped

4 large garlic cloves, coarsely chopped

1-inch/2.5-cm piece fresh ginger, coarsely chopped

4 tbsp sunflower oil or olive oil

1 tsp ground cumin

1 tsp ground coriander

$1/2$ tsp ground fennel

1 tsp ground turmeric

$1/2$–1 tsp chili powder

6 oz/175 g canned chopped tomatoes

14 oz/400 g canned black-eyed peas, drained and rinsed

4 oz/115 g large flat mushrooms, wiped and cut into bite-size pieces

$1/2$ tsp salt, or to taste

$3/4$ cup warm water

1 tbsp chopped fresh mint

1 tbsp chopped fresh cilantro leaves

Indian bread, to serve

method

1 Process the onion, garlic, and ginger in a food processor or blender.

2 Heat the oil in a medium pan over medium–high heat and add the processed ingredients. Cook for 4–5 minutes, then add the cumin, coriander, fennel, turmeric, and chili powder. Stir-fry for about 1 minute, then add the tomatoes. Cook until the tomatoes are pulpy and the juice has evaporated.

3 Add the black-eyed peas, mushrooms, and salt. Stir well and pour in the warm water, then bring to a boil, cover the pan, and reduce the heat to low. Simmer for 8–10 minutes, stirring halfway through.

4 Stir in the chopped mint and cilantro and remove from the heat. Transfer to a serving dish and serve with Indian bread.

lentils with fresh chiles, mint & cilantro

ingredients

SERVES 4

1/3 cup split red lentils (masoor dhal)

1/3 cup skinless split chickpeas (channa dhal)

3 tbsp sunflower oil or olive oil

1 onion, finely chopped

2 tsp garlic paste

2 tsp ginger paste

2–3 fresh green chiles, chopped (seeded if you like)

1 tsp ground cumin

2 1/2 cups warm water

1 tsp salt, or to taste

1 tbsp chopped fresh mint

1 tbsp chopped fresh cilantro leaves

4 tbsp unsalted butter

1 fresh green chile and 1 small tomato, seeded and cut into julienne strips, to garnish

method

1 Wash both types of lentil together until the water runs clear and let soak for 30 minutes.

2 Heat the oil in a medium saucepan, preferably nonstick, over medium heat and add the onion, garlic paste, ginger paste, and chiles. Stir-fry the mixture until it begins to brown.

3 Drain the lentils and add to the onion mixture together with the cumin. Reduce the heat to low and stir-fry for 2–3 minutes, then pour in the warm water. Bring to a boil, reduce the heat to low, cover, and simmer for 25–30 minutes.

4 Stir in the salt, mint, cilantro, and butter. Stir until the butter has melted, then remove from the heat. Serve garnished with the strips of chile and tomato.

mixed lentils with five-spice seasoning

ingredients

SERVES 4

generous 1/2 cup split red lentils (masoor dhal)

generous 1/2 cup skinless split mung beans (mung dhal)

3 3/4 cups water

1 tsp ground turmeric

1 tsp salt, or to taste

1 tbsp lemon juice

2 tbsp sunflower oil or olive oil

1/4 tsp black mustard seeds

1/4 tsp cumin seeds

1/4 tsp nigella seeds

1/4 tsp fennel seeds

4–5 fenugreek seeds

2–3 dried red chiles

1 small tomato, seeded and cut into strips, and fresh cilantro sprigs, to garnish

Indian bread, to serve

method

1 Mix the lentils and beans together and wash until the water runs clear. Place the water in a saucepan over medium heat, bring to a boil, then add the lentils and beans. Bring to a boil, then reduce the heat slightly. Boil for 5–6 minutes, and when the foam subsides, add the turmeric, reduce the heat to low, cover, and cook for 20 minutes. Add the salt and lemon juice and beat the dhal with a wire whisk, adding a little more hot water if the dhal is too thick.

2 Heat the oil in a small saucepan over medium heat. When hot, but not smoking, add the mustard seeds. As soon as they begin to pop, reduce the heat to low and add the cumin seeds, nigella seeds, fennel seeds, fenugreek seeds, and dried chiles. Let the spices sizzle until the seeds begin to pop and the chiles have blackened. Pour the contents of the pan over the lentils, scraping off all the residue from the bottom of the pan.

3 Turn off the heat and keep the pan covered until you are ready to serve. Transfer to a serving dish and garnish with tomato strips and cilantro sprigs. Serve with Indian bread.

tarka dhal

ingredients

SERVES 4

1 cup split red lentils
(masoor dhal)

3$^1/_2$ cups water

1 tsp salt, or to taste

2 tsp sunflower oil or olive oil

$^1/_2$ tsp black or brown
mustard seeds

$^1/_2$ tsp cumin seeds

4 shallots, finely chopped

2 fresh green chiles, chopped
(seeded if you like)

1 tsp ground turmeric

1 tsp ground cumin

1 fresh tomato, chopped

2 tbsp chopped fresh cilantro
leaves

method

1 Wash the lentils until the water runs clear and put into a medium saucepan. Add the water and bring to a boil. Reduce the heat to medium and skim off the foam. Cook, uncovered, for 10 minutes. Reduce the heat to low, cover, and cook for 45 minutes, stirring occasionally to ensure that the lentils do not stick to the bottom of the pan as they thicken. Stir in the salt.

2 Meanwhile, heat the oil in a small saucepan over medium heat. When hot, but not smoking, add the mustard seeds, followed by the cumin seeds. Add the shallots and chiles and cook, stirring, for 2–3 minutes, then add the turmeric and cumin. Add the tomato and cook, stirring, for 30 seconds.

3 Fold the shallot mixture into the cooked lentils. Stir in the cilantro, remove from the heat, and serve immediately.

kitchri

ingredients

SERVES 4–6

scant 1¹/₄ cups basmati rice

2 tbsp ghee, vegetable oil,
    or peanut oil

1 large onion, finely chopped

1¹/₄ cups red split lentils
    (masoor dhal), rinsed

2 tsp garam masala

1¹/₂ tsp salt, or to taste

pinch of ground asafetida

3¹/₂ cups water

2 tbsp chopped fresh cilantro

chapatis and raita, to serve

method

1 Rinse the basmati rice in several changes of water until the water runs clear, then let soak for 30 minutes. Drain and set aside until ready to cook.

2 Melt the ghee in a flameproof casserole or large pan with a tight-fitting lid over medium–high heat. Add the onion and sauté for 5–8 minutes, stirring frequently, until golden but not browned.

3 Stir in the rice and lentils along with the garam masala, salt, and asafetida, and stir for 2 minutes. Pour in the water and bring to a boil, stirring.

4 Reduce the heat to as low as possible and cover the pan tightly. Simmer without lifting the lid for 20 minutes, until the grains are tender and the liquid is absorbed. Re-cover the pan, turn off the heat, and let stand for 5 minutes.

5 Use 2 forks to mix in the cilantro and adjust the seasoning, adding more salt if necessary. Serve with chapatis and raita.

egg & lentil curry

ingredients

SERVES 4

3 tbsp ghee or vegetable oil

1 large onion, chopped

2 garlic cloves, chopped

1-inch/2.5-cm piece fresh
   ginger, chopped

$1/2$ tsp minced fresh chile or
   chili powder

1 tsp ground coriander

1 tsp ground cumin

1 tsp paprika

$1/3$ cup red split lentils
   (masoor dhal)

$1^{3}/_{4}$ cups vegetable stock

8 oz/225 g canned chopped
   tomatoes

6 eggs

$1/2$ cup coconut milk

2 tomatoes, cut into wedges

salt

fresh cilantro sprigs,
   to garnish

chapatis, to serve

method

1 Melt the ghee in a saucepan, add the onion, and fry gently for 3 minutes. Stir in the garlic, ginger, chile, and spices and cook gently, stirring frequently, for 1 minute. Stir in the lentils, stock, and tomatoes and bring to a boil. Reduce the heat, cover, and let simmer, stirring occasionally, for 30 minutes, until the lentils are tender.

2 Meanwhile, place the eggs in a saucepan of cold water and bring to a boil. Reduce the heat and let simmer for 10 minutes. Drain and cover immediately with cold water.

3 Stir the coconut milk into the lentil mixture and season well with salt. Process the mixture in a blender or food processor until smooth. Return to the pan and heat through.

4 Shell the hard-cooked eggs and cut into wedges. Divide between 4 serving dishes. Arrange a tomato wedge between each egg wedge. Spoon the hot lentil sauce over the eggs and tomatoes, adding enough to flood the plate. Garnish with cilantro sprigs and serve hot with chapatis.

snacks &
accompaniments

Tasty snacks are a way of life in India and, in the West, will make a delightful change from potato chips or nuts served with predinner drinks. More substantial treats, such as samosas (deep-fried pastry parcels) and onion bhajis (crisp onion fritters) make great appetizers, unusual lunches, and fabulous party fare.

Rice is always served with Indian meals, often just plainly boiled. More elaborate rice dishes with herbs, spices, nuts, and other ingredients are served on special occasions. The most popular type of rice is basmati, a fragrant long-grained variety that is grown in the foothills of the Himalayas. If you have time, rinse it in several changes of cold water and let soak for 30 minutes before cooking.

Bread is almost as essential to a meal as rice and is prepared daily in Indian homes. Authentic flat bread is surprisingly quick and easy to make, and even the yeast dough for slipper-shaped naan requires little effort and time, apart from letting it rise.

A wonderfully contrasting mixture of tastes and textures characterizes an Indian meal and this is further enhanced with a variety of savory chutneys and relishes. Whether a cooling yogurt-based raita or a hot lime pickle, these flavorsome accompaniments add the final touch of perfection.

vegetable samosas

ingredients

MAKES 12

3 tbsp sunflower oil or olive oil

$1/2$ tsp black mustard seeds

1 tsp cumin seeds

1 tsp fennel seeds

1 onion, finely chopped

2 fresh green chiles, finely
  chopped (seeded if
  you like)

2 tsp ginger paste

$1/2$ tsp ground turmeric

1 tsp ground coriander

1 tsp ground cumin

$1/2$ tsp chili powder

12 oz/350 g boiled potatoes,
  cut into bite-size pieces

scant 1 cup frozen peas,
  defrosted

1 tsp salt, or to taste

2 tbsp chopped fresh cilantro
  leaves

12 sheets filo dough, about
  11 x 7 inches/28 x 18 cm

4 tbsp butter, melted, plus
  extra for greasing

chutney, for serving

method

1 Heat the oil in a saucepan over medium heat and add the mustard seeds, followed by the cumin and fennel seeds. Add the onion, chiles, and ginger paste and cook, stirring frequently, for 5–6 minutes.

2 Add the ground spices and cook, stirring, for 1 minute. Add the potatoes, peas, and salt and stir until the vegetables are thoroughly coated with the spices. Stir in the cilantro and remove from the heat. Let cool completely.

3 Preheat the oven to 350°F/180°C and line a baking sheet with parchment paper.

4 Place a sheet of filo dough on a board and brush well with the melted butter. Keep the remaining filo dough sheets covered with a moist cloth or plastic wrap. Fold the buttered filo dough sheet in half lengthwise, brush with some more melted butter, and fold lengthwise again.

5 Place about 1 tablespoon of the vegetable filling on the bottom right-hand corner of the filo dough sheet and fold over to form a triangle. Continue folding to the top of the sheet, maintaining the triangular shape. Transfer to the prepared baking sheet and brush with melted butter. Repeat with the remaining sheets of filo dough and filling.

6 Bake in the preheated oven for 20 minutes, or until browned. Serve hot with chutney.

onion bhajis

ingredients

SERVES 4

generous 1 cup chickpea
    flour

1 tsp salt, or to taste

small pinch of baking soda

$1/4$ cup ground rice

1 tsp fennel seeds

1 tsp cumin seeds

2 fresh green chiles, finely
    chopped (seeded if
    you like)

2 large onions, about 14 oz/
    400 g, sliced into half-rings
    and separated

1 cup fresh cilantro, including
    the tender stalks, finely
    chopped

scant 1 cup water

sunflower oil or olive oil,
    for deep-frying

tomato or mango chutney,
    to serve

method

1 Sift the chickpea flour into a large bowl and add the salt, baking soda, ground rice, and fennel and cumin seeds. Mix together thoroughly, then add the chiles, onions, and cilantro. Gradually pour in the water and mix until a thick batter is formed and all the other ingredients are thoroughly coated with it.

2 Heat enough oil for deep-frying in a wok, deep saucepan, or deep-fat fryer over medium heat to 350°F/180°, or until a cube of bread browns in 30 seconds. If the oil is not hot enough, the bhajis will be soggy. Add as many small amounts (about $1/2$ tablespoon) of the batter as will fit in a single layer, without overcrowding. Reduce the heat slightly and cook the bhajis for 8–10 minutes, until golden brown and crisp.

3 Remove and drain on paper towels. Keep hot in a low oven while you cook the remaining batter.

4 Serve hot with chutney.

savory cheese cakes

ingredients

MAKES 8

2 large slices day- or two-day-old white bread, crusts removed

8 oz/225 g paneer, provolone cheese, or firm tofu (drained weight), grated

3 shallots, finely chopped

1 tsp fennel seeds

$1/2$ tsp cumin seeds

1 tbsp chopped fresh mint leaves or $1/2$ tsp dried mint

2 tbsp chopped fresh cilantro leaves

1 tsp ginger paste

$1/4$ cup slivered almonds, lightly crushed (optional)

1 fresh green chile, chopped (seeded if you like)

$1/2$ tsp garam masala

$1/2$ tsp chili powder (optional)

$1/2$ tsp salt, or to taste

1 tbsp lemon juice

1 large egg, beaten

sunflower oil or vegetable oil, for pan-frying

method

1 Soak the bread slices in a bowl of water for 1–2 minutes, then squeeze out all the water and crumble the slices between your palms. Put the bread in a large bowl and add all the remaining ingredients, except the oil. Mix well to form a binding consistency.

2 Divide the mixture in half and shape each half into 4 equal-size flat cakes $1/4$ inch/ 5 mm thick.

3 Pour oil into a skillet to a depth of 1 inch/ 2.5 cm and heat over medium heat. Add the cakes and cook for 5 minutes on each side, or until well browned. Drain on paper towels and serve hot.

golden cauliflower pakoras

ingredients

SERVES 4

vegetable oil or peanut oil,
    for deep-frying
4 cups cauliflower florets
chutney, to serve

batter

1 cup chickpea flour
2 tsp ground coriander
1 tsp garam masala
1 tsp salt
$1/2$ tsp ground turmeric
pinch of chili powder
1 tbsp ghee, melted, or
    vegetable oil or peanut oil
1 tsp lemon juice
$2/3$ cup cold water
2 tsp nigella seeds

method

1 To make the batter, stir the chickpea flour, coriander, garam masala, salt, turmeric, and chili powder into a large bowl. Make a well in the center, add the ghee and lemon juice with 2 tablespoons of the water, and stir together to make a thick batter.

2 Slowly beat in enough of the remaining water with an electric handheld mixer or a whisk to make a smooth batter about the same thickness as heavy cream. Stir in the nigella seeds. Cover the bowl and let stand for at least 30 minutes.

3 When you are ready to cook, heat enough oil for deep-frying in a kadhai, wok, deep-fat fryer, or large heavy-bottom pan until it reaches 350°F/180°C, or until a cube of bread browns in 30 seconds. Dip one cauliflower floret at a time into the batter and let any excess batter fall back into the bowl, then drop it into the hot oil. Add a few more dipped florets, without overcrowding the pan, and cook for about 3 minutes, or until golden brown and crisp.

4 Use a slotted spoon to remove the fritters from the oil and drain well on crumpled paper towels. Continue cooking until all the cauliflower florets and batter have been used. Serve the hot fritters with chutney for dipping.

sweet & spicy nuts

ingredients

SERVES 6–8

$1^1/_2$ cups superfine sugar

1 tsp sea salt

2 tbsp mild, medium, or hot
curry powder, to taste

1 tsp ground turmeric

1 tsp ground coriander

pinch of chili powder

3 cups mixed whole
blanched almonds
and shelled cashew nuts

vegetable oil or peanut oil,
for deep-frying

method

1 Mix the sugar, salt, curry powder, turmeric, coriander, and chili powder together in a large bowl, then set aside.

2 Meanwhile, bring a large pan of water to a boil. Add the almonds and cashews and blanch for 1 minute, then pour them into a strainer to drain and shake off as much of the excess water as possible. Immediately toss the nuts with the sugar and spices.

3 Heat enough oil for deep-frying in a wok, deep-fat fryer, or large heavy-bottom pan to 350°F/180°C, or until a cube of bread browns in 30 seconds. Use a slotted spoon to remove the nuts from the spice mixture, leaving the spice mixture behind in the bowl, then drop the nuts into the hot oil. Cook them for 3–4 minutes, stirring occasionally and watching carefully because they can burn quickly, until they turn golden.

4 Remove the nuts from the oil with the slotted spoon and toss them in the remaining spice mixture. Pour the nuts into a strainer and shake off the excess spices, then let cool completely—they should be crispy. Store in an airtight container for up to a week.

bhel poori

ingredients

SERVES 4

$10^1/2$ oz/300 g new potatoes

7 oz/200 g canned
     chickpeas, rinsed and very
     well drained

$3^1/2$ oz/100 g sev noodles

2 oz/55 g puffed rice

4 tbsp raisins

2 tbsp chopped fresh cilantro

1 tbsp fennel seeds, toasted
     and cooled

pooris, crushed
     (see page 192)

salt

chaat masala

1 tbsp coriander seeds

1 tbsp cumin seeds

1 tsp black peppercorns

2 dried red chiles

to serve

plain yogurt

tamarind chutney
     (see page 206)

cilantro chutney
     (see page 198)

method

1 Bring a large pan of salted water to a boil and cook the potatoes for 12–15 minutes, until tender. Drain and run under cold water to cool, then peel and cut into 1/4-inch/5-mm dice. Cover and let chill for at least 30 minutes.

2 Meanwhile, to make the chaat masala, heat a dry skillet over high heat. Add the coriander and cumin seeds, peppercorns, and chiles and stir around until they give off their aroma. Immediately turn them out of the pan to stop them from cooking, watching closely because the cumin seeds burn quickly. Grind the toasted spice mixture in a spice grinder or with a pestle and mortar.

3 Use your hands to toss together the potatoes, chickpeas, sev noodles, puffed rice, raisins, cilantro, fennel seeds, and crushed pooris. Sprinkle with the chaat masala and toss again.

4 Divide the mixture among small serving bowls or place in one large bowl and drizzle with the yogurt and chutneys to taste. It is best eaten straight away so it doesn't become soggy.

plantain chips

ingredients

SERVES 4

4 ripe plantains

1 tsp mild, medium, or hot
curry powder, to taste

vegetable oil or peanut oil,
for deep-frying

mango chutney, to serve

method

1 Peel the plantains, then cut crosswise into
1/8-inch/3-mm slices. Put the slices in a bowl,
sprinkle over the curry powder, and use your
hands to toss them lightly together.

2 Heat enough oil for deep-frying in a wok,
deep-fat fryer, or large heavy-bottom pan to
350°F/180°C, or until a cube of bread browns
in 30 seconds. Add as many plantain slices as
will fit in the pan without overcrowding and
cook for 2 minutes, or until golden.

3 Remove the plantain chips from the pan with
a slotted spoon and drain well on crumpled
paper towels. Serve hot with mango chutney.

spiced basmati rice

ingredients

SERVES 4–6

scant 1¼ cups basmati rice

2 tbsp ghee, vegetable oil,
    or peanut oil

5 green cardamom pods,
    bruised

5 cloves

½ cinnamon stick

1 tsp fennel seeds

½ tsp black mustard seeds

2 bay leaves

2 cups water

1½ tsp salt, or to taste

2 tbsp chopped fresh cilantro

pepper

method

1 Rinse the basmati rice in several changes of water until the water runs clear, then let soak for 30 minutes. Drain and set aside until ready to cook.

2 Melt the ghee in a flameproof casserole or a large saucepan with a tight-fitting lid over medium–high heat. Add the spices and bay leaves and stir for 30 seconds. Stir the rice into the casserole so the grains are coated with ghee. Stir in the water and salt and bring to a boil.

3 Reduce the heat to as low as possible and cover the casserole tightly. Simmer, without lifting the lid, for 8–10 minutes, until the grains are tender and all the liquid is absorbed.

4 Turn off the heat and use two forks to mix in the cilantro. Adjust the seasoning, adding salt and pepper if necessary. Re-cover the pan and let stand for 5 minutes.

mint & cilantro rice with toasted pine nuts

ingredients

SERVES 4

good pinch of saffron threads, pounded

2 tbsp hot milk

generous 1 cup basmati rice

2 tbsp sunflower oil or olive oil

2-inch/5-cm piece cinnamon stick, broken in half

4 green cardamom pods, bruised

2 star anise

2 bay leaves

2 cups lukewarm water

3 tbsp fresh cilantro leaves, finely chopped

2 tbsp fresh mint leaves, finely chopped, or 1 tsp dried mint

1 tsp salt, or to taste

scant 1/4 cup pine nuts

method

1 Soak the pounded saffron threads in the hot milk and set aside until you are ready to use. Wash the rice in several changes of cold water until the water runs clear. Let soak in fresh cold water for 20 minutes, then let drain in a colander.

2 Heat the oil in a medium heavy-bottom saucepan over low heat. Add the cinnamon, cardamom, star anise, and bay leaves and let sizzle gently for 20–25 seconds. Add the rice and stir well to ensure that the grains are coated with the flavored oil.

3 Add the water, stir once, and bring to a boil. Add the saffron and milk, cilantro, mint, and salt and boil for 2–3 minutes. Cover tightly, reduce the heat to very low, and cook for 7–8 minutes. Turn off the heat and let stand, covered, for 7–8 minutes.

4 Meanwhile, preheat a small heavy-bottom skillet over medium heat, add the pine nuts, and cook, stirring, until lightly toasted. Alternatively, cook in a foil-covered broiler pan under a preheated medium broiler, turning 2–3 times, until lightly toasted. Transfer to a plate and let cool.

5 Add half the toasted pine nuts to the rice and fluff up the rice with a fork. Transfer to a serving dish, garnish with the remaining pine nuts, and serve immediately.

lemon-laced basmati rice

ingredients

SERVES 4

generous 1 cup basmati rice

2 tbsp sunflower oil or olive oil

$1/2$ tsp black or brown
   mustard seeds

10–12 curry leaves,
   preferably fresh

scant $1/4$ cup cashews

$1/4$ tsp ground turmeric

1 tsp salt, or to taste

2 cups hot water

2 tbsp lemon juice

1 tbsp snipped fresh chives,
   to garnish

method

1 Wash the rice in several changes of cold water until the water runs clear. Let soak in fresh cold water for 20 minutes, then let drain in a colander.

2 Heat the oil in a nonstick saucepan over medium heat. When hot, but not smoking, add the mustard seeds, followed by the curry leaves and the cashews (in that order).

3 Stir in the turmeric, quickly followed by the rice and salt. Cook, stirring, for 1 minute, then add the hot water and lemon juice. Stir once, bring to a boil, and boil for 2 minutes. Cover tightly, reduce the heat to very low, and cook for 8 minutes. Turn off the heat and let stand, covered, for 6–7 minutes.

4 Fork through the rice and transfer to a serving dish. Garnish with the chives and serve immediately.

fruit & nut pilaf

ingredients

SERVES 4–6

scant 1¼ cups basmati rice

2 cups water

½ tsp saffron threads

1 tsp salt, or to taste

2 tbsp ghee, vegetable oil,
   or peanut oil

generous ⅓ cup blanched
   almonds

1 onion, thinly sliced

1 cinnamon stick, broken in
   half

seeds from 4 green
   cardamom pods

1 tsp cumin seeds

1 tsp black peppercorns,
   lightly crushed

2 bay leaves

3 tbsp finely chopped dried
   mango

3 tbsp finely chopped dried
   apricots

2 tbsp golden raisins

generous ⅓ cup pistachios,
   chopped

method

1 Rinse the basmati rice in several changes of water until the water runs clear, then let soak for 30 minutes. Drain and set aside until ready to cook.

2 Boil the water in a small pan. Add the saffron threads and salt, remove from the heat, and set aside to steep.

3 Melt the ghee in a flameproof casserole or large pan with a tight-fitting lid over medium–high heat. Add the almonds and stir them around until golden brown, then immediately use a slotted spoon to scoop them out of the casserole.

4 Add the onion to the casserole and sauté, stirring frequently, for 5–8 minutes, until golden but not browned. Add the spices and bay leaves to the pan and stir them around for about 30 seconds.

5 Add the rice to the casserole and stir until the grains are coated with ghee. Add the saffron-steeped water and bring to a boil. Reduce the heat to as low as possible, stir in the dried fruits, and cover the casserole tightly. Simmer, without lifting the lid, for 8–10 minutes, until the grains are tender and all the liquid is absorbed.

6 Turn off the heat and use 2 forks to mix the almonds and pistachios into the rice. Adjust the seasoning, adding more salt if necessary. Re-cover the pan and let stand for 5 minutes.

spiced basmati pilaf

ingredients

SERVES 4

2$^1/_2$ cups basmati rice

6 oz/175 g head of broccoli

6 tbsp vegetable oil

2 large onions, chopped

8 oz/225 g button
   mushrooms, sliced

2 garlic cloves, crushed

6 green cardamom pods,
   bruised

6 whole cloves

8 black peppercorns

1 cinnamon stick or piece of
   cassia bark

1 tsp ground turmeric

5 cups boiling vegetable stock
   or water

$^1/_3$ cup seedless raisins

$^1/_2$ cup unsalted pistachios,
   coarsely chopped

salt and pepper

method

1 Place the rice in a strainer and wash well under cold running water. Drain. Trim off most of the broccoli stalk and cut into small florets, then quarter the stalk lengthwise and cut diagonally into 1-cm/$^1/_2$-inch pieces.

2 Heat the oil in a large pan. Add the onions and broccoli stalks and cook over low heat, stirring frequently, for 3 minutes. Add the mushrooms, rice, garlic, and spices and cook for 1 minute, stirring, until the rice is coated in oil.

3 Add the boiling stock and season to taste with salt and pepper. Stir in the broccoli florets and return the mixture to a boil. Cover, reduce the heat, and cook over low heat for 15 minutes without uncovering the pan.

4 Remove the pan from the heat and let the pilaf stand for 5 minutes without uncovering. Remove the whole spices, add the raisins and pistachios, and gently fork through to fluff up the grains. Serve the pilaf hot.

chapatis

ingredients

MAKES 16

scant 3 cups chapati flour
(atta), plus extra for
dusting

1 tsp salt

1/2 tsp granulated sugar

2 tbsp sunflower oil or olive oil

generous 1 cup lukewarm
water

method

1 Mix the chapati flour, salt, and sugar together in a large bowl. Add the oil and work well into the flour mixture with your fingertips. Gradually add the water, mixing at the same time. When the dough is formed, transfer to a counter and knead for 4–5 minutes. The dough is ready when all the excess moisture is absorbed by the flour. Alternatively, mix the dough in a food processor. Wrap the dough in plastic wrap and let rest for 30 minutes.

2 Divide the dough in half, then cut each half into 8 equal-size pieces. Form each piece into a ball and flatten into a round cake. Dust each cake lightly in the flour and roll out to a 6-inch/15-cm circle. Keep the remaining cakes covered while you are working on one. The chapatis will cook better when freshly rolled out, so roll out and cook one at a time.

3 Preheat a heavy-bottom cast-iron griddle (tawa) or a large heavy-bottom skillet over medium–high heat. Put a chapati on the griddle and cook for 30 seconds. Using a thin spatula, turn over and cook until bubbles begin to appear on the surface. Turn over again. Press the edges down gently with a clean cloth to encourage the chapati to puff up—they will not always puff up, but this doesn't matter. Cook until brown patches appear on the underside. Remove from the pan and keep hot by wrapping in a piece of foil lined with paper towels. Repeat with the remaining dough cakes.

chile-cilantro naan

ingredients

MAKES 8

3¼ cups all-purpose flour

2 tsp sugar

1 tsp salt

1 tsp baking powder

1 egg

generous 1 cup milk

2 tbsp sunflower oil or olive
oil, plus extra for oiling

2 fresh red chiles, chopped
(seeded if you like)

1 cup fresh cilantro leaves,
chopped

2 tbsp butter, melted

method

1 Sift the flour, sugar, salt, and baking powder together into a large bowl. Whisk the egg and milk together, then gradually add to the flour and mix until a dough is formed.

2 Transfer the dough to a counter, make a depression in the center of the dough, and add the oil. Knead for 3–4 minutes, until you have a smooth and pliable dough. Wrap the dough in plastic wrap and let rest for 1 hour.

3 Divide the dough into 8 equal-size pieces, form each piece into a ball, and flatten into a thick cake. Cover the dough cakes with plastic wrap and let rest for 10–15 minutes.

4 Preheat the broiler to high. Line a broiler pan with foil and brush with oil.

5 Roll each flattened cake into a 5-inch/13-cm circle and pull the lower end gently. Carefully roll out again, maintaining the teardrop shape, to about 9 inches/23 cm in diameter.

6 Mix the chiles and cilantro together, then spread on the surface of the naans. Press gently so that the mixture sticks to the dough. Transfer a naan to the prepared broiler pan and cook for 1 minute, or until slightly puffed and brown patches appear on the surface. Turn over and cook the other side for 45–50 seconds, until lightly browned. Remove from the broiler and brush with the melted butter. Wrap in a dish towel while you cook the remaining naans.

pooris

ingredients

MAKES 12

1¹/₂ cups whole-wheat flour,
    sifted, plus extra for
    dusting

¹/₂ teaspoon salt

2 tbsp ghee, melted

¹/₃–²/₃ cup water

vegetable oil or peanut oil,
    for deep-frying

method

1 Put the flour and salt into a bowl and drizzle the ghee over the surface. Gradually stir in the water until a stiff dough forms.

2 Turn out the dough onto a lightly floured counter and knead for 10 minutes, or until it is smooth and elastic. Shape the dough into a ball and place it in a clean bowl, then cover with a damp dish towel and let rest for 20 minutes.

3 Divide the dough into 12 equal-size pieces and roll each into a ball. Working with one ball of dough at a time, flatten the dough between your palms, then thinly roll it out on a lightly floured counter into a 5-inch/13-cm circle. Continue until all the dough balls are rolled out.

4 Heat at least 3 inches/7.5 cm oil in a wok, deep-fat fryer, or large skillet until it reaches 350°F/180°C, or until a cube of bread browns in 30 seconds. Drop a poori into the hot oil and deep-fry for about 10 seconds, or until it puffs up. Use 2 large spoons to flip the poori over and spoon some hot oil over the top.

5 Use the 2 spoons to lift the poori from the oil and let any excess oil drip back into the pan. Drain the poori on crumpled paper towels and serve immediately. Continue until all the pooris are cooked, making sure the oil returns to the correct temperature before you add another poori.

cucumber raita

ingredients

SERVES 4–5

1 small cucumber

$^3/_4$ cup plain yogurt

$^1/_4$ tsp sugar

$^1/_4$ tsp salt

1 tsp cumin seeds

10–12 black peppercorns

$^1/_4$ tsp paprika

method

1 Peel the cucumber and scoop out the seeds. Cut the flesh into bite-size pieces and set aside.

2 Put the yogurt in a bowl and beat with a fork until smooth. Add the sugar and salt and mix well.

3 Preheat a small heavy-bottom saucepan over medium–high heat. When the pan is hot, turn off the heat and add the cumin seeds and peppercorns. Stir for 40–50 seconds, until they release their aroma. Remove from the pan and let cool for 5 minutes, then crush in a mortar with a pestle or on a hard surface with a rolling pin.

4 Set aside $^1/_4$ teaspoon of this mixture and stir the remainder into the yogurt. Add the cucumber and stir to mix.

5 Transfer the raita to a serving dish and sprinkle with the reserved toasted spices and the paprika.

mint & spinach chutney

ingredients

SERVES 4–6

2 oz/55 g tender fresh
  spinach leaves

3 tbsp fresh mint leaves

2 tbsp chopped fresh cilantro
  leaves

1 small red onion, coarsely
  chopped

1 small garlic clove, chopped

1 fresh green chile, chopped
  (seeded if you like)

2$^1/_2$ tsp granulated sugar

1 tbsp tamarind juice or juice
  of $^1/_2$ lemon

method

1 Put all the ingredients in a blender or food processor and blend until smooth, adding a little water to enable the blades to move, if necessary.

2 Transfer to a serving bowl, cover, and chill in the refrigerator for at least 30 minutes.

cilantro chutney

ingredients

SERVES 4–6

1¹/₂ tbsp lemon juice

1¹/₂ tbsp water

3 oz/85 g fresh cilantro leaves
and stems, coarsely
chopped

2 tbsp chopped fresh coconut

1 small shallot, very finely
chopped

¹/₄-inch/5-mm piece fresh
ginger, chopped

1 fresh green chile, seeded
and chopped

¹/₂ tsp sugar

¹/₂ tsp salt

pinch of pepper

method

1 Put the lemon juice and water in a small food processor, add half the cilantro, and process until it is blended and a slushy paste forms. Gradually add the remaining cilantro and process until it is all blended, scraping down the sides of the processor, if necessary. If you don't have a processor that will cope with this small amount, use a pestle and mortar, adding the cilantro in small amounts.

2 Add the remaining ingredients and continue blending until they are all finely chopped and blended. Taste and adjust any of the seasonings, if you like. Transfer to a nonmetallic bowl, cover, and chill for up to 3 days before serving.

onion & tomato salad

ingredients

SERVES 4

3 tomatoes, seeded and
  chopped

1 large onion, finely chopped

3 tbsp chopped fresh cilantro,
  plus extra to garnish

1–2 fresh green chiles,
  seeded and very finely
  sliced

2 tbsp lemon juice, or to taste

1 tsp salt, or to taste

pinch of sugar

pepper

method

1 Put the tomatoes, onion, cilantro, and chiles in a bowl. Add the lemon juice, salt, sugar, and pepper to taste, then gently toss all together. Cover and chill for at least 1 hour.

2 Just before serving, gently toss the salad again. Add extra lemon juice or salt and pepper to taste. Spoon into a serving bowl and sprinkle with chopped cilantro.

coconut sambal

ingredients

SERVES 4

$^{1}/_{2}$ fresh coconut or $1^{1}/_{4}$ cups
dry unsweetened coconut

2 fresh green chiles, chopped
(seeded if you like)

1-inch/2.5-cm piece fresh
ginger, peeled and finely
chopped

4 tbsp chopped fresh cilantro

2 tbsp lemon juice, or to taste

2 shallots, very finely chopped

method

1 If you are using a whole coconut, use a hammer and nail to punch a hole in the "eye" of the coconut, then pour out the water from the inside and reserve. Use the hammer to break the coconut in half, then peel half and chop.

2 Put the coconut and chiles in a food processor and process for about 30 seconds, until finely chopped. Add the ginger, cilantro, and lemon juice and process again.

3 If the mixture seems too dry, stir in about 1 tablespoon of the reserved coconut water. Stir in the shallots and serve immediately, or cover and chill until required.

mango chutney

ingredients

SERVES 4–6

1 large mango, about 14 oz/ 400 g, peeled, pitted, and finely chopped

2 tbsp lime juice

1 tbsp vegetable oil or peanut oil

2 shallots, finely chopped

1 garlic clove, finely chopped

2 fresh green chiles, seeded and finely sliced

1 tsp black mustard seeds

1 tsp coriander seeds

5 tbsp grated jaggery or light brown sugar

5 tbsp white wine vinegar

1 tsp salt

pinch of ground ginger

method

1 Put the mango in a nonmetallic bowl with the lime juice and set aside.

2 Heat the oil in a large skillet or pan over medium–high heat. Add the shallots and sauté for 3 minutes. Add the garlic and chiles and stir for an additional 2 minutes, or until the shallots are softened but not browned. Add the mustard seeds and coriander seeds, then stir.

3 Add the mango to the pan with the jaggery, vinegar, salt, and ginger and stir. Reduce the heat to its lowest setting and simmer for 10 minutes, until the liquid thickens and the mango becomes sticky.

4 Remove from the heat and let cool completely. Transfer to an airtight container, cover, and chill for 3 days before using.

tamarind chutney

ingredients

SERVES 4–6

3$\frac{1}{2}$ oz/100 g tamarind pulp, chopped

2 cups water

$\frac{1}{2}$ fresh Thai chile, or to taste, seeded and chopped

generous $\frac{1}{4}$ cup light brown sugar, or to taste

$\frac{1}{2}$ tsp salt, or to taste

method

1 Put the tamarind and water in a heavy-bottom saucepan over high heat and bring to a boil. Reduce the heat to the lowest setting and simmer for 25 minutes, stirring occasionally to break up the tamarind pulp, or until tender.

2 Put the tamarind pulp into a strainer and use a wooden spoon to push the pulp into the rinsed-out pan.

3 Stir in the chile, sugar, and salt and continue simmering for an additional 10 minutes, or until the desired consistency is reached. Let cool slightly, then stir in extra sugar or salt to taste.

4 Let cool completely, then cover tightly and chill for up to 3 days, or freeze.

lime pickle

ingredients

SERVES 6–8

12 limes, halved and seeded

4 oz/115 g salt

2¹/₂ oz/70 g chili powder

1 oz/25 g mustard powder

1 oz/25 g ground fenugreek

1 tbsp ground turmeric

1¹/₄ cups mustard oil

¹/₂ oz/15 g yellow mustard
    seeds, crushed

¹/₂ tsp asafetida

method

1 Cut each lime half into 4 pieces and pack them into a large sterilized jar, sprinkling over the salt at the same time. Cover and let stand in a warm place for 10–14 days, or until the limes have turned brown and softened.

2 Mix the chili powder, mustard powder, fenugreek, and turmeric together in a small bowl and add to the jar of limes. Stir to mix, then re-cover and let stand for 2 days.

3 Transfer the lime mixture to a heatproof bowl. Heat the oil in a heavy-bottom skillet. Add the mustard seeds and asafetida to the skillet and cook, stirring continuously, until the oil is very hot and just starting to smoke.

4 Pour the oil and spices over the limes and mix well. Cover and let cool. When cool, pack into a sterilized jar. Seal and store in a sunny place for a week before serving.

desserts & drinks

Most of us would agree that there can be little more delicious after a hot, spicy main course than a palate-cleansing fruit dish or refreshing iced dessert. Indian-style ice cream, especially with a tropical flavor, is a must-try treat. It's worth noting, too, that it is easier to make at home than western-style ice cream. Indian cooks are also aware that milk has a cooling effect and use it as the basis for a number of popular desserts, from rich rice dessert to halva, an intensely flavored, fudgelike sweetmeat. Indian desserts are perfect for those with a sweet tooth and are special enough to serve to guests at the end of any meal, whether Indian or western.

Tea has been grown in India since the first half of the nineteenth century. It remains a favorite beverage and is served in a variety of ways, including flavored with a mix of spices. It is not the only popular drink, however, and is rivaled by the yogurt-based lassi. Sweet and savory versions are sold at roadside stalls, served in restaurants, and made at home to refresh, cool, and, it is thought, to aid digestion. Finally, we include recipes for cooling citrus-based syrups—the perfect thirst-quenchers at the end of a long, hot summer's day.

mango kulfi

ingredients

SERVES 6–8

generous 1¹/₂ cups canned
    evaporated milk
1¹/₄ cups light cream
¹/₄ cup ground almonds
¹/₂–¹/₃ cup granulated sugar
1 lb/450 g mango puree
1 tsp freshly ground
    cardamom seeds
scant ¹/₄ cup shelled unsalted
    pistachios, to decorate

method

1 Pour the evaporated milk and cream into a heavy-bottom saucepan and stir to mix. Put over medium heat. Mix the ground almonds and sugar together, then add to the milk mixture. Cook, stirring, for 6–8 minutes, until the mixture thickens slightly.

2 Remove from the heat and let the mixture cool completely, stirring from time to time to prevent a skin from forming. When completely cold, stir in the mango puree and ground cardamom.

3 Meanwhile, preheat a small saucepan over medium heat, add the pistachios, and toast for 2–3 minutes. Let cool, then lightly crush. Store in an airtight container until required.

4 Kulfi is set in traditional conical-shape plastic or steel molds, which you can buy from Asian stores, but you can use decorative individual molds or popsicle molds instead. Fill the containers of your choice with the kulfi mixture and freeze for 5–6 hours. Transfer the kulfi to the refrigerator for 40 minutes, then invert onto serving dishes. Serve sprinkled with the crushed pistachios to decorate.

indian rice dessert

ingredients

SERVES 4

good pinch of saffron threads, pounded
2 tbsp hot milk
3 tbsp ghee or unsalted butter
generous $1/2$ cup ground rice
$1/4$ cup slivered almonds
scant $1/4$ cup seedless raisins
$2 1/2$ cups whole milk
2 cups evaporated milk
$1/4$ cup superfine sugar
12 plumped dried apricots, sliced
1 tsp freshly ground cardamom seeds
$1/2$ tsp freshly grated nutmeg
2 tbsp rose water

to decorate

$1/4$ cup walnut pieces
2 tbsp shelled unsalted pistachios

method

1 Place the pounded saffron in the hot milk and let soak until needed.

2 Set aside 2 teaspoons of the ghee and melt the remainder in a heavy-bottom saucepan over low heat. Add the ground rice, almonds, and raisins and cook, stirring, for 2 minutes. Add the whole milk, increase the heat to medium, and cook, stirring, until it begins to bubble gently. Reduce the heat to low and cook, stirring frequently, for 10–12 minutes, to prevent the mixture from sticking to the bottom of the pan.

3 Add the evaporated milk, sugar, and apricots, setting a few slices aside to decorate. Cook, stirring, until the mixture thickens to the consistency of a pouring custard.

4 Add the reserved saffron and milk mixture, cardamom, nutmeg, and rose water, stir to distribute well, and remove from the heat. Let cool, then cover and chill in the refrigerator for at least 2 hours.

5 Melt the reserved ghee in a small saucepan over low heat. Add the walnuts and cook, stirring, until they brown a little. Remove and drain on paper towels. Brown the pistachios in the saucepan, remove, and drain on paper towels. Let the pistachios cool, then lightly crush.

6 Serve the dessert decorated with the fried nuts and the reserved apricot slices.

sago & coconut dessert

ingredients

SERVES 4

$1/2$ fresh coconut

1 cup water

$3^1/2$ cups milk

scant $1/2$ cup superfine sugar

2 tbsp raisins

scant $1/3$ cup sago

seeds from 6–8 green
    cardamom pods

$1/4$ cup slivered almonds,
    to decorate

method

1 To prepare the coconut milk, remove the flesh from the coconut shell and grate it. Place in a food processor or blender, add the water, and process until smooth. Strain into a pitcher, pressing down on the coconut with the back of a wooden spoon. Discard the contents of the strainer and reserve the coconut milk.

2 Bring the $3^1/2$ cups milk to a boil in a large heavy-bottom pan and continue to boil until it has reduced to $2^1/2$ cups. Reduce the heat, add the sugar, and stir until dissolved. Stir in the raisins and sago. Let simmer gently for 6–8 minutes, or until the sago is cooked.

3 Remove the pan from the heat and stir in the coconut milk and cardamom seeds, then pour into individual serving dishes. Sprinkle with the almonds and let cool before serving.

almond sherbet

ingredients

SERVES 2

scant 1^1/$_2$ cups whole
   almonds
2 tbsp sugar
1^1/$_4$ cups milk
1^1/$_4$ cups water

method

1 Soak the almonds in a large bowl of water for at least 3 hours, or preferably overnight.

2 Using a sharp knife, chop the almonds into small pieces. Grind to a fine paste in a food processor or with a mortar and pestle.

3 Add the sugar to the almond paste and grind again to make a fine paste. Add the milk and water and mix well (in a blender if you have one).

4 Transfer the almond sherbet to a large serving dish. Let chill in the refrigerator for 30 minutes. Stir the almond sherbet just before serving.

almond & pistachio dessert

ingredients

SERVES 2

5^1/$_2$ tbsp unsalted butter

2 cups ground almonds

1 cup sugar

^{2}/$_3$ cup light cream

8 almonds, chopped

10 pistachios, chopped

method

1 Melt the butter in a heavy-bottom pan, preferably nonstick, stirring well. Add the ground almonds, sugar, and cream, stirring well. Reduce the heat and stir constantly for 10–12 minutes, scraping the bottom of the pan.

2 Increase the heat until the mixture turns a little darker in color.

3 Transfer the almond mixture to a large, shallow serving dish and smooth the top with the back of a spoon.

4 Decorate the top of the dessert with the chopped almonds and pistachios. Let set for 1 hour, then cut into diamond shapes and serve cold.

carrot halva

ingredients

SERVES 4–6

4 tbsp ghee or unsalted
    butter
1-inch/2.5-cm piece
    cinnamon stick, halved
$1/4$ cup slivered almonds
scant $1/4$ cup cashews
scant $1/4$ cup seedless raisins
8 carrots, grated
$2^1/2$ cups whole milk
scant $3/4$ cup superfine sugar
$1/2$ tsp freshly ground
    cardamom seeds
$1/2$ tsp freshly grated nutmeg
$1/4$ cup heavy cream
2 tbsp rose water
vanilla ice cream or whipped
    heavy cream, to serve

method

1 Melt the ghee in a heavy-bottom saucepan over low heat. Add the cinnamon stick and let sizzle gently for 25–30 seconds. Add the almonds and cashews and cook, stirring, until lightly browned. Remove about a dessertspoon of the nuts and set aside.

2 Add the raisins, carrots, milk, and sugar to the saucepan, increase the heat to medium, and bring the milk to boiling point. Continue to cook over low–medium heat for 15–20 minutes, until the milk evaporates completely, stirring frequently, and scraping and blending in any thickened milk that sticks to the side of the saucepan. Don't allow any milk that is stuck to the side to brown or burn, because this will give the dessert an unpleasant flavor.

3 Stir in the cardamom, nutmeg, cream, and rose water. Remove from the heat and let cool slightly, then serve topped with a scoop of vanilla ice cream or whipped heavy cream. Sprinkle over the reserved nuts to decorate.

shrikhand with pomegranate

ingredients

SERVES 4

4 cups plain yogurt

$1/4$ tsp saffron threads

2 tbsp milk

generous $1/4$ cup superfine
   sugar, or to taste

seeds from 2 green
   cardamom pods

2 pomegranates or other
   exotic fruit

method

1 Line a strainer set over a bowl with a piece of cheesecloth large enough to hang over the edge. Add the yogurt, then tie the corners of the cheesecloth into a tight knot and tie them to a faucet. Let the bundle hang over the sink for 4 hours, or until all the excess moisture drips away.

2 Put the saffron threads in a dry pan over high heat and "toast," stirring frequently, until you can smell the aroma. Immediately turn them out of the pan. Put the milk in the pan, return the saffron threads, and warm just until bubbles appear around the edge, then set aside and let steep.

3 When the yogurt is thick and creamy, put it in a bowl, stir in the sugar, cardamom seeds, and saffron-and-milk mixture, and beat until smooth. Taste and add extra sugar, if desired. Cover and chill for at least 1 hour, until well chilled.

4 Meanwhile, to prepare the pomegranate seeds, cut the fruit in half and use a small teaspoon or your fingers to scoop out the seeds.

5 To serve, spoon the yogurt into individual bowls or plates and add the pomegranate seeds.

ginger ice cream with date & tamarind sauce

ingredients

SERVES 4–5

4 cups vanilla ice cream

2 tsp ground ginger

7 oz/200 g candied ginger, chopped, to serve

tamarind sauce

$1/3$ cup seedless raisins

$1/2$ cup pitted dried dates

generous 1 cup boiling water

2 rounded tsp tamarind concentrate or 3 tbsp tamarind juice

scant $1/4$ cup molasses sugar

method

1 Let the ice cream stand at room temperature for 35–40 minutes to soften, then transfer to a bowl. Add the ground ginger and beat well. Return the mixture to the carton and freeze for 3–4 hours.

2 Meanwhile, to make the sauce, put the raisins and dates in a heatproof bowl, pour over the boiling water, and let soak for 15–20 minutes. Transfer to a food processor, add the tamarind and sugar, and blend to a smooth paste. Transfer to a nonmetallic bowl and let cool.

3 Put scoops of the ice cream into serving dishes and drizzle over the sauce. Arrange 1 dessertspoon of candied ginger on top of each dessert and serve immediately. Serve any extra sauce separately.

spiced fruit salad

ingredients

SERVES 4–6

finely grated rind and juice of
   1 lime

1 lb/450 g fresh fruits, such
   as bananas, guavas,
   oranges, kumquats,
   mangoes, melons, and
   pineapple

yogurt, to serve

spiced syrup

$1^{1}/_{4}$ cups superfine sugar

$^{2}/_{3}$ cup water

1 vanilla bean, sliced
   lengthwise

1 cinnamon stick, broken in
   half

$^{1}/_{2}$ tsp fennel seeds

$^{1}/_{2}$ tsp black peppercorns,
   lightly crushed

$^{1}/_{2}$ tsp cumin seeds

method

1 Begin by making the spiced syrup. Put the sugar, half the water, the vanilla bean, cinnamon stick, fennel seeds, peppercorns, and cumin seeds into a small heavy-bottom pan over medium–high heat. Slowly bring to a boil, stirring to dissolve the sugar. As soon as the sugar boils, stop stirring and let the syrup bubble until it turns a golden brown.

2 Stand back from the pan and stir in the remaining water: the syrup will splash and splatter. Stir again to dissolve any caramel, then remove the pan from the heat and let the syrup cool slightly.

3 Meanwhile, put the lime rind and juice in a large heatproof bowl. Prepare and cut each fruit as required and add it to the bowl. If you are using bananas, toss them immediately in the lime juice to prevent discoloration.

4 Pour in the syrup and let the fruits and syrup cool completely, then cover the bowl and chill for at least 1 hour before serving with thick, creamy yogurt.

salt lassi

ingredients

SERVES 4–6

3 cups plain yogurt

$1/2$ tsp salt

$1/4$ tsp sugar

generous 1 cup water

ice cubes

ground cumin and fresh mint
    sprigs, to decorate

method

1 Beat the yogurt, salt, and sugar together in a pitcher or bowl, then add the water and whisk until frothy.

2 Fill 4–6 glasses with ice cubes and pour over the yogurt mixture. Lightly dust the top of each glass with ground cumin and decorate with mint sprigs.

mango lassi

ingredients

SERVES 4–6

1 large mango, about
  10$\frac{1}{2}$ oz/300 g, peeled,
  pitted, and coarsely
  chopped
3 cups plain yogurt
generous 1 cup cold water
about 2 tbsp superfine sugar,
  or to taste
fresh lime juice, to taste
ice cubes
ground ginger, to decorate
  (optional)

method

1 Put the mango in a food processor or blender with the yogurt and process until smooth. Add the water and process again to blend.

2 The amount of sugar you will add depends on how sweet the mango is. Taste and stir in sugar to taste, then stir in the lime juice.

3 Fill 4–6 glasses with ice cubes and pour over the mango mixture. Lightly dust the top of each glass with ground ginger, if you like.

masala tea

ingredients

SERVES 4–6

4 cups water

1-inch/2.5-cm piece fresh
   ginger, coarsely chopped

1 cinnamon stick

3 green cardamom pods,
   bruised

3 cloves

1 1/2 tbsp Assam tea leaves

sugar and milk, to taste

method

1 Pour the water into a heavy-bottom pan over medium–high heat. Add the ginger, cinnamon stick, cardamom, and cloves and bring to a boil. Reduce the heat and simmer for 10 minutes.

2 Put the tea leaves in a teapot and pour over the water and spices. Stir and let steep for 5 minutes.

3 Strain the tea into teacups and add sugar and milk to taste.

ginger refresher

ingredients

SERVES 4-6

2^1/$_2$ oz/70 g fresh ginger,
very finely chopped

^{1}/$_2$ tbsp finely grated lemon
rind

5 cups boiling water

2 tbsp fresh lemon juice,
or to taste

4 tbsp superfine sugar,
or to taste

lemon slices and fresh mint
sprigs, to decorate

method

1 Put the ginger in a heatproof bowl with the lemon rind. Pour over the boiling water, stir, and let steep overnight.

2 Strain the liquid into a large pitcher. Stir in the lemon juice and sugar, stirring until the sugar dissolves. Taste and add extra lemon juice and sugar, if you like. Serve decorated with lemon slices and mint sprigs.

lime cooler

ingredients

SERVES 4

generous ¹/₂ cup superfine
    sugar

5 tbsp freshly squeezed lime
    juice

1 tsp finely chopped fresh
    mint, plus extra sprigs
    to decorate

4 cups water

crushed ice, to serve

method

1 Place the sugar, lime juice, and chopped mint in a large bowl and stir in the water until the sugar has dissolved.

2 Cover the bowl with plastic wrap and let chill in the refrigerator for 3–4 hours.

3 Strain the mixture into a pitcher, discarding the contents of the strainer. Fill tall glasses with crushed ice and pour in the lime mixture. Decorate with mint sprigs and serve immediately.